Barbed Wire and Rice

B. D. McKendree

Army recruit B.D. McKendree in San Francisco, March, 1941,
just before leaving for the Philippines.

Barbed Wire and Rice

Poems and Songs From Japanese Prisoner-of-War Camps

Collected by
Bishop D. McKendree

East Asia Program
Cornell University
Ithaca, New York 14853

The Cornell East Asia Series is published by the Cornell University East Asia Program and is not affiliated with Cornell University Press. We are a small, non-profit press, publishing reasonably priced books on a wide variety of topics relating to East Asia as a service to the academic community and the general public. We accept standing orders which may be cancelled at any time and which provide for automatic billing and shipping of each title in the series upon publication.

If after review by internal and external readers a manuscript is accepted for publication, it is published on the basis of camera-ready copy provided by the volume author. Each author is thus responsible for any necessary copy-editing and for manuscript formatting. Submission inquiries should be addressed to Editorial Board, East Asia Program, Cornell University, Ithaca, New York 14853-7601.

© 1995 by Bishop Davis McKendree. All rights reserved
ISSN 1050-2955
ISBN 0-939657-77-5 cloth
ISBN 0-939657-75-9 paper
Printed in the United States of America

Contents

Foreword

Bishop McKendree's gathering of songs and poems from the Japanese prisoner of war camps of World War II is a remarkable outcome to a brutal experience.

The materials were elusive in their circulation among the prisoners, dangerous to those who composed or performed them, and certainly would have been fatal to McKendree, had he been caught with them.

They tell their stories, and Bishop McKendree his, in this book. Rather than retelling, or trying in some way to add emphasis to that story here, I wish to point out a few noteworthy features of poetry and song illustrated by this collection. First, poetry and songs give refuge for the individual who is working on their composition, and a sense of solidarity among those who hear, perform, or record them. The Russian poet Osip Mandelstam, in the prison house of 1920s Russia, composed a short, satirical poem on Joseph Stalin which fell into the wrong hands, or the wrong ear. For that one poem, Mandelstam was doomed to a labor camp where he died, near Vladivostok. His poem was a simple, crude satire, making fun of Stalin's fat (but lethal) fingers.

That same fun at the expense of the prisoners' overseers—who at any moment could, and too often did execute a prisoner for some infraction—provides the occasion, in several of the songs and poems in this collection, for a sardonic laugh. Share the joke with another, and the isolation of combat, or imprisonment, is relieved momentarily.

Songs and poems become a medium for political counter-statement. The soldiers taken prisoner with Bishop McKendree were war prisoners, but at the same time, political prisoners, used by their

Japanese captors to represent political statements about Japanese superiority.

The Japanese guards subjected their prisoners to a constant campaign of disrespect. Songs and poems, in that environment, become counter-statements, like the extended middle fingers of each one of the Pueblo crewmen in the photograph taken and distributed by their North Korean captors at the time of the Pueblo incident in 1968. Songs and poems and middle-finger gestures are a form of political sabotage.

Songs and poems give a place of formal order, sequence, repetition, and of expectations raised and fulfilled. As the poet Robert Frost observed, poetry acts as a momentary stay against confusion, and through just such a momentary stay, the prisoners recovered brief control of their situation from the guards and the prison camp system.

Songs and poems are a spell, transforming outward reality by bending it to a simple, inner logic of rhyme, meter, and verse, and by subjecting the feared or resented, more powerful, guards to the private mockeries of puns and scatological humor.

These songs and poems will also tell the reader something of what their authors, composers, singers—and scribe—lived through. We can sense, but dimly, certain of the details of the physical environment, the personalities of the prisoners and of the guards, and the events which brought them together. These songs and poems will summon forth, for those who were there, a sense of common purpose and experience, of shared hope and despair, defeat and accomplishment; for other readers—and my earnest wish is to have this book find its way to Japanese readers, too—a sense of honor, compassion and respect.

These songs and poems have also occasioned the story about his own life which I asked Bishop McKendree to add to this collection so that I and other readers might have a better sense of who he is and how he came to take on the responsibility of writing down and saving these materials. On that basis, he wrote about growing up in the small town of Vega in the Texas Panhandle, about enlisting, and going off to war. I trust that his fellow soldiers, as well as younger generations like my own and others to follow, will find his story an interesting one.

Bishop's wife, Beverly, at a gathering in early July of 1994 at my parents' home in Newton, Massachusetts, spent a few minutes writing something down on a slip of paper which she then handed to me. I will end the brief Foreword with her list, to remind us.

List of Bishop's decorations:
Silver Star
Bronze Star
Purple Heart
Ex-POW Medal
Good Conduct
American Defense
Asiatic-Pacific Theatre
WW II Victory
Philippine Defense
Philippine Independence
Presidential Unit Citation with Two Oak Leaf Clusters
Philippine Presidential Unit Citation
Seven Overseas Service Stripes

David R. McCann
Cornell University

Preface

The poems in this book were written by men who were confined in Japanese prison camps during World War II and, with few exceptions, served on either Bataan or Corregidor in the defense of the Philippines against the Japanese aggressors who invaded the Islands immediately after the sneak attack on Pearl Harbor.

In the misery and boredom of prison life, men would search for ways to relieve the monotony and to occupy their time. Anyone who could obtain a writing instrument and something to write on would spend some time writing. Some men would spend time torturing themselves by writing down names of, and recipes for, all the delicious food they could remember or imagine. (It is very hard for one to keep his mind off food when he is constantly hungry.) Other men would keep diaries or collect names and addresses of friends and acquaintances in prison camp. However, some men were creative enough to put some of their thoughts into poetry, and they are the source of this work. Since I am not a writer, I concentrated on collecting the poems written by others. I committed to memory some of the ones I thought were best in case my copies were destroyed.

These poems were collected from various men in the prison camps. I copied them down on can labels and any other scraps of paper I could find to write on. In most cases, the poems had been passed from person to person to the extent that the identity of the author was lost. I have given credit in all cases when I obtained the poem from the author or when the name was still known and given to me.

Please bear in mind that the men who wrote these poems represent a very wide spectrum of social, economic, and educational backgrounds. Probably most of the men who composed these poems did not survive until the end of the war since so many men died while in the custody of the Japanese.

Just before I was shipped from the Philippines in October of 1944 on one of the infamous "death ships," I obtained a paper cement sack which consisted of several layers of brown paper. The cement bag and I managed to survive the thirty-nine days of extreme misery, torture, and suffering on the Haro Maru (which we dubbed the "Benjo Maru," *benjo* being the Japanese word for latrine) and disembarked on Taiwan* in November, 1944. While on Taiwan, I had time to make a booklet using the paper sack and I recopied all the poems from the scraps of paper to the booklet. Fortunately, the booklet has survived until this time and has been donated to the Barker Texas History Center Archives at the University of Texas at Austin.

My wife, son, and two daughters have each suggested at various times that I publish the poems and write the story of my war experience. As a result of these suggestions, I got to thinking that it is likely that I have the only copy of most of these poems in existence today. Since the one copy could be destroyed by fire or storm at any time, I decided to make an effort to have copies made. My wife and daughters volunteered to prepare a booklet of the poems. After much effort, a booklet was made and copies were given to a few of our friends. It was as a result of this distribution that the manuscript was presented to the editorial board of the Cornell East Asia Program.

While these poems may not be outstanding literary examples, I think some of them are very good; that they have historical and social value, if not artistic merit; and that they are worth preserving.

This work is dedicated to those men, living and dead, who wrote these poems, and I hope their message will be understood and appreciated.

---

* We knew Taiwan as Formosa at that time.

Acknowledgments

I wish to express my sincere thanks and appreciation to the following persons for making this book possible:

My wife, Beverly, for her work in arranging and helping with the typing of the initial draft and preparing the table of contents. Her many hours of work in putting the autobiography, foreword, and preface into the computer and making many corrections and additions in the final preparation for printing of this book are appreciated.

My daughters, Jean and Edith, for the great amount of time they spent typing various drafts of this collection and continuing to compile and edit the manuscript of the poems into a computer to obtain the final result.

My son, Alan, for all of the time he has spent helping with the computer, and for doing all of the formatting to make the camera-ready copy. I also thank him for the use of his laser printer. Without his help and technical expertise it would not have been possible for us to prepare the final copy.

Dr. David McCann of Cornell University for his interest when he read the collection of poems, his advice and guidance in preparing the autobiography, and for presenting the manuscript to Cornell's editorial board for their consideration.

Dr. Carol MacKay, professor of English at UT Austin, and our good friend, for her patient and unfailing advice and support while I was writing the autobiography and for proof-reading the manuscript.

My sister-in-law, Roberta Biery, for her help and encouragement and for proofreading the manuscript.

Helen and Richard McCann, our dear friends, who initiated the chain of events which led to the publication of this book by showing a copy of the poems to their son, David.

The editorial board of the Cornell East Asia Program for their consideration of this manuscript and assistance in its preparation.

Our many good friends in Austin and elsewhere who have provided support and encouragement over a long period of time.

I

Poems from Prison Camps

"An advance guard
with no main body . . ."

Vindication

[From an article published in 1939: *The younger generation, that is, the war babies now reaching maturity, seem utterly incapable of taking on the responsibilities of the nation. They are aimless, soft, and generally immature.*]

They said we were soft; we were aimless;
They said we were spoiled past reclaim;
We had lost the "American Spirit";
We were blots on America's name.

We were useless—weaklings and drifters,
And the last youth census reveals
We had lost the "faith of our fathers";
We had sacrificed muscles for wheels.

The old men wept for their country
And sighed for the days of yore.
And somehow we half believed them,
But that was before the war.

Before we had heard the bomb shriek
And the howling so ugly and shrill
That ripples over the cane fields
When the Nippy comes in for the kill.

Before we had lived on hunger
And rumors and nerves and pain.
Before we had seen our buddies
Dying among the cane.

Our war! Our own little rat trap;
The helpless defense of Bataan.
An advance guard with no main body,
Yet a thorn in the side of Japan.

So now we can laugh at our elders,
And now we can give them the lie.
We held the line that couldn't be held
When they struck at Abucay.

Soft? Weaklings? And aimless?
Go where the steel was sowed;
Ask of the endless fox groves
That dot the "Hacienda Road."

And ask at the tangled thickets,
Deadly and green and hot,
And the bloody Pilar river
And the forward slopes of Samat.

Ask at Limay and Balanga
Where the outposts burrowed like moles;
Where the sky-trained flying soldiers
Died in the infantry's holes.

And last seek the silent jungles
Where the unburied bodies lie
Asleep by their rusted rifles—
The men who learned how to die.

Who squeezed the Garand's trigger?
Who met the tanks on a mare?

Who flew the primary trainers
When Zeros were in the air?

Who watched the bomb bays open
Day after endless day?
Who stayed by their anti-aircraft
With tons of H.E. on the way?

Who led the scouts at Quinauan?
Who stopped the break at Moran?
Who, but the immature youngsters,
The forgotten men of Bataan?

So now we have learned our lesson
And how to apply it, too,
And this is the application—
The things that they said were true.

We were soft—weaklings and aimless.
We believed in ourselves alone,
But now we are tempered with fire;
We're ready, U.S., to come home.

Motors in the west

The old man with the whiskers
Was pointing straight at me.
He said, "Your country needs you,"
So I signed up for three.

The recruiting sergeant told me
Of a life that was the best,
But not a word was said that day
About "Motors in the west."

He spoke to me in dulcet tones
As to a man of means.
"Travel's what you need," he said.
"Why not try the Philippines?"

So now I am here; the war is on;
I never would have guessed
That this small phrase would mean so much;
"Flash! Motors in the west."

There was a time here on "The Rock"
When all was hope and cheer.
Our main concern was how to pay
Our monthly bill for beer.

But the club was bombed, the beer is gone.
We're in our bomb proofs pressed,
Quiet! Silence! There it goes again.
"Flash! Motors in the west."

9

Somewhere the sun is shining;
Somewhere there is rest;
But there is peace no more on Corregidor;
There are "Motors in the west."

But MacArthur's men will carry on,
And each will do his best
To throw a great big monkey wrench
In those "Motors in the west."

— Wills

Corregidor Mac

From out of his hole, four stories below,
Came courageous Corregidor Mac,
With a one-five-five to keep him alive
And a howitzer strapped to his back.

I'll ride through Bataan as fast as I can.
Rest assured; I am practically back.
I'll feed them carabao steak and rice pattie cake
And keep the potatoes for Mac.

I'll tell Franklin D. of all that I see
And probably more to boot;
Of the skies being black when our bombers attack,
And once more the bull I can shoot.

So get my Chris-Craft ready; I am a bit unsteady,
For I had a busy day on the line.
I want to get back to my underground shack.
Brother Quezon is ready to dine.

The Fall of Corregidor

Constantly pounded, day and night,
On this fastness, men did fight.
Rather than destroy them all,
Ruined Corregidor must fall.
Every man in his own way
Gave his best fight here today.
In the memory of those who died
Defending this, their country's pride
While there on the beaches now turned red,
Rugged soldier boys lie dead.

I witnessed the scene which inspired the following poem. As the poem states, it was the morning after the formal surrender of all troops on Corregidor.

We had destroyed our weapons on the day of the surrender, but due to the confused situation that day, and due to the continued bombing and sporadic shelling, those of us in the area not yet occupied by the Japanese troops remained under cover as best we could until the following morning when all firing had ceased.

After we had been concentrated near Malinta Tunnel on the west side of Malinta Hill, the Japanese decided to march us around the south side of the hill and on out to an area we called the "92nd Garage Area." As we were marching out to that area, we marched through a part where some of the last fighting took place, and where there were still many dead bodies. Since they had been lying in the tropical sun for almost two days, you can imagine their condition.

As we rounded a bend in the road, there was the body which inspired this poem. The soldier was still sitting behind his thirty-caliber machine gun. There was a small hill or mound behind him, so that when he was hit, he fell back against the mound in such a way that it propped him up, one arm raised slightly above his head. It is hard to imagine how he died in that position, but he did, and this grisly sight inspired the author to write the poem. I do not know who wrote it or if he survived the prison camps.

The Unknown Soldier

The morning after the surrender
We were trooping o'er the hill.
The sound of trampling, tired feet
Broke the unaccustomed still.

The weary eyes of the men that morn
Saw a sight not soon forgot
Of broken guns and broken men
Whose bodies were left to rot.

I saw the corpse of a youngster;
Just a lad, too young to die.
One blackened arm was raised
And pointed to the sky.

Where are you pointing, soldier?
What message would you give?
What are you trying to tell us,
The ones who are left to live?

Do you point to that place called home
That lies beyond the sea,
That place which meant so much to you
Which you never again shall see?

Or do you point to where you have gone,
To that far-off, golden shore
Where men can live as brothers
And there isn't any war?

Or are you trying to tell us,
As o'er the hill we plod,
To raise our minds from killing
And lift our thoughts to God?

Well, we must march on and leave you,
Just a pile of flesh and bone.
You may be better off than we,
For our fate is yet unknown.

In twenty years when a maddened world
Is ready to fight again,
We'll remember that upraised, pointing arm;
Perhaps we'll heed your message then.

"A brave little band . . ."

The Bastards of Bataan

We have no fathers, but we do not care;
No mothers anywhere.
We have no Uncle Sam at all;
Just the same, we'll never fall,
The Bastards of Bataan.

Miracle men, our fame did spread;
Miracle men whom the Japs did dread.
A brave little band, both near and far,
But to the Japs, we always are
The Bastards of Bataan.

We drink, and fight to drink again,
A toast to those whose lives did end
When the Japs chose to strike
A band of men who could fight,
The Bastards of Bataan.

We live on rice and carabao;
We fight and fight, though God knows how,
Mid tropical fevers running high
Causing brave, strong men to die,
The Bastards of Bataan.

We live on pain, to hope to fly.
We pray and pray, to live, to cry,
But our shattered dreams and pains
Have gained us nought, save despair.
The Bastards of Bataan.

We must fight on another day
For our convoy's on the way.
It will be in Manila's bay
To help us save the fight some way,
The Bastards of Bataan.

"Wainwright's Warriors" when MacArthur fled;
"Wainwright's Warriors" when half are dead;
Always fighting without a grumble
Until the last defense has crumbled,
The Bastards of Bataan.

Surrender! Throw down your arms;
Return to our stores and farms,
So we go back to our occupations
Which we know have long been taken,
But not by the Bastards of Bataan.

Peace at last to a troubled world;
Homeward bound to our best girl;
While to a draft dodger she was wed,
While on Bataan her soldier bled,
A Bastard of Bataan.

Strikes, and taxes, tariffist talk,
Will destroy the weak and disgust the brave.
Communism, Socialism, and Nazism too,
With life and living, I am through.
I'll go west with the Bastards of Bataan.

A Soldier Boy

The airplanes ceased their bombing;
The field guns stood grim and still.
The smoke and haze of battle
Hung low over distant hill.

The sun was sinking slowly;
Its golden rays shone down
Upon the dead and dying
On the bloody battleground.

And one, among the dying,
A youth, not yet a man,
Who was drafted from his happy home
To fight in old Bataan.

His brother knelt beside him
As his life blood ebbed away,
And bent his head in pity
To hear what he might say.

The dying brother looked up
And whispered, "Brother Jack,
Take this message to our mother
If ever you get back."

Jack's tears again fell fast
As he clasped his brother's hand
And listened to the message
He must take back from Bataan.

"Tell Mother how I died
On Bataan's wide battlefield
Where bullets rained so thickly
And flashing steel met steel.

"Tell her how they promised
They would send us planes and men
And tell her how we waited
For ships that never came in.

"This hope was always burning
In the heart of every man
But at last we knew it was hopeless
For the boys of old Bataan.

"Tell her how we lived
With only rice to eat,
Some boiled coconut and banana stalks,
And sometimes a little carabao meat.

"Tell her not to weep for me
For waiting I will stand
At the golden gate of Heaven—
Her boy from old Bataan.

"And there's another, brother Jack,
That little fair-haired girl.
I'm sure that she is waiting
On the other side of the world.

"She kissed me as we parted,
And whispered, 'Goodbye, Pat,

I'll be waiting here at home
In this town when you get back.'

"So, brother, take this trinket,
'Tis but a golden band,
To my sweetheart who is waiting
For her soldier from old Bataan.

"So raise me up, dear brother,
So I may see the setting sun
Gleaming on the 'Stars and Stripes'
Before the day is done."

He saluted the flag so slowly;
A tear stood in each eye
As he said, "Farewell, Old Glory,
It's not so hard to die.

"Beneath your silken folds
I never more shall stand,
So farewell, Old Glory, mother, brother,
My sweetheart, and old Bataan."

His brother saw him falter
And laid him gently back,
And heard him softly whisper,
"I must leave you now, dear Jack."

He saw his eyelids quiver
As they closed so very slow;
He realized that his brother
Was here on earth no more.

Oh, God, receive his lonely soul;
It's the end of life's short span.
The brother of my childhood
Has died in old Bataan.

That night, the pale moon rose
And calmly, it shone down
Upon a solemn funeral
On Bataan's battleground.

His buddies offered up a prayer
There beneath the mango tree
And someone sang that sweet old song,
"Nearer, My God, To Thee."

The bamboos seemed to bow their heads
There in that war-torn land
While the soldier boy was laid to rest
In a grave in old Bataan.

Old Bataan

Ole Franklin came before the house
And gave a fireside chat.
He said we'd win this bloody war;
We've got it in the hat.

He said that we'd have victory
Just for you and me
But said, "You'll have to wait, my friend,
'Til nineteen forty-three."

He said we had a navy;
The finest in the world,
But with the obsolete guns they've got,
They couldn't kill a squirrel.

It was down in old Pearl Harbor
That the Japs began to bomb,
And since that awful mess they made,
We've all been on the run.

They took me out to Frisco Bay
Back in forty-one.
They put me on a transport boat
And said, "So long, you son-of-a-gun."

I sailed the ole Pacific
And landed in ole Bataan,
And now, my friends, I'll tell you
The kind of guy I am.

I'm a hungry man from old Bataan.
There's nothing in the pot.
I guess I'm just a soldier boy
The nation has forgot.

Ole Franklin says, "I love you;
Now boys, you know I do,
But until I break the navy's neck,
There's nothing I can do."

The War Department said, "Now, men,
You mustn't be alarmed;
There's nothing in the old Far East
To do you any harm."

And then the enemy airplanes came.
They'll kill you if they can.
We almost tore the road up
Going to ole Bataan.

Now we're the Battling Bastards of Bataan;
We're mighty rough and tough.
We fought like hell with what we had,
But that was not enough.

So come on, you Yanks, and hurry up,
And send some help this way;
So we can set that Rising Sun
That's shining every day.

Bataan

The jungles of Bataan are quiet now;
No longer torn by bomb or shell.
White crosses in the jungle gloom
Show where tortured bodies fell.

Exotic orchids grace the jungle's tallest trees
Birds of gorgeous plumage fill the air with song.
Yet white crosses mutely speak;
"Dear God, ours was not the wrong."

We fell, the dust was red like wine
With blood from tortured flesh and bone.
We died; to dust returned our mortal clay,
Our souls winged upward home.

The "spirit" no bomb or shell can conquer,
Lies not where tortured bodies fell.
Lead on, our comrades, bravely fallen
Where men are beasts and earth is hell.

Bataan Blues

Oh, we are near Mariveles Mountain
In the province of Bataan.
We've stopped old Tojo in his tracks;
We're better man for man.
The papers say help is on the way,
But, gosh, where is that man?
We've looked for Yanks for many weeks
With salmon in our pans.

P-Forties play near Subic Bay
As they daily take the air.
Old Tojo, in a wild report,
Said fifty-two were there.
Now if four P-Forties
Can multiply in flight,
Maybe a convoy of one boat
Might start an awful fight.

Now if the Yanks want back Luzon
As a base against Japan,
Just clean up Java some dark night
And we'll fix a place to land.
Just shake the lead out over there;
We'll use it over here.
We've lived on rice and fish too long,
Please, convoy, bring us beer.

The birds will sing of MacArthur's men
And the battles of Bataan.

They fought the Japs from north to south;
They withdrew, but never ran.
They hunted the Japs both day and night
In holes and up in trees,
But the little devils were
As elusive as the breeze.

We had lots of messages
By pamphlets in the air,
But before we ever had them read,
The bombers too are there.
They offer "Co-prosperity"
In the Asiatic sphere.
They said, "This war is not for you.
We love you, brother dear."

They sunk our barge of cigarettes,
And said, "So sorry, Joe,
But if you don't give up real quick,
It's in the drink you go."
The Thirty-first* said great big words;
"You'll never hurt us yet.
We'll hang your hide in Tokyo;
On that you sure can bet."

Oh, there are D.S.C.'s and S.S.C.'s,
And glory for the taking,
But give me a ride on a great big boat,
And I'll stop my belly-aching.

---

* Refers to the 31st regiment, the only regular infantry regiment on Bataan that was all mainland U.S. soldiers.

April Ninth, '42

A bloody day, I say to you,
That ninth of April, forty-two
When we had been pushed back to shore
Beyond which lay Corregidor
Across the channels in the bay.
Her guns were silent as if to say,
"You fought them hard, we know you're there,
Our guns would help if we knew where,
But jungles hide you, we know,
And we might hit friend instead of foe."
Bataan surrendered, hope had gone
And left "The Rock" to carry on.
She arose to make one final thrust,
And then fell back 'midst blood and dust.
You fought in jungle, mountain, plain;
You fought for life, it seems, in vain.
You learned to dodge both bomb and shell;
You learned to laugh when life was hell;
You learned to fight without a gun;
You learned to stick and never run.
You're tired and hungry, with sleepless nights,
Those jungle trails, Manila's lights;
A gun that's jammed, a screaming man,
His guts ripped out; a burning flare;
A crippled tank that hit a mine,
A heavy hit and weakened line;
A field piece split right to the breach,
A landing boat high on a beach;

A plane that fell and failed to rise,
Its pilot dead with staring eyes;
A sniper hid up in a tree
Observing, looking, hard to see;
The setting sun, a flash of steel,
A guarded match, a flashing light.
They must attack, no moon tonight.
A whispered challenge, "Foe or friend?"
Good God! this night will never end.
Where is the help? We're nearly done.
The line is breaking, can't reform.
We're falling back; how long 'til morn?
"The C.P., please," must stop this rout.
"I'm sorry, sir, the line is out."
A flag of truce unfurled to breeze;
A gallant force brought to its knees.
And slowly came the realization;
No cheer of joy, and no elation.
They had done their best, the going was rough.
Their best was good, but not good enough.

Battling Boys of Bataan

When the gates of hell are open well,
And the devil does all he can;
There sit those souls upon the coals,
The Battling Boys of Bataan.

Then the devil goes high in the sky
To interview St. Pete.
He's full of charm in his uniform;
His horns are all shining and neat.

"St. Pete," says he, "How can it be?
Those souls have called my bluff.
I've turned the heat up to the peak,
But they are much too tough.

"They won't brown, or even frown,
Or ask for the water can.
What shall I do with such a crew,
Those Battling Boys of Bataan?"

Says Pete, "I surmise," while looking wise,
"To deal with such a clan,
They won't even fright at all your might,
They've had their hell on Bataan.

"You must give to me, as you can see,
Their keeping at this point.
They fought well while in that hell
And now deserve this joint."

Which?

We've heard much talk and a little tattle
Of who's to blame for losing the battle.
There's the Philippine army, so quick to retreat,
Our own clipped-wing air corps, our own flat feet,
Our noble-like leader deep down in the tunnel
Who considers himself a way above Rommel.
But most to blame, we all agree,
Are the Medical Corps and the Q.M.C.

Bombs, bullets, mines are the weapons of war.
But in tropical climes, more dangerous by far
And more to be feared, as everyone knows,
Is the lethal end of a mosquito's nose.
So there in the place where anopheles whine,
Who do you think ran short of quinine?
I'll give you one guess; you shouldn't need more.
Not the Q.M.C., but the Medical Corps.

As Macaulay once said, every school boy knows,
It is not on its feet that the army goes.
If you want it to fight, you must fill its belly
Three full times a day; first meal at reveille.
So who in Bataan, where the tropical heat
Is such that even the strong feel weak,
Considered two rice meals are sufficient for me?
Not the Medical Corps, but the Q.M.C.

Of all the dread sounds I hear in Bataan,
The one I hate most is the wounded's "Ward man!"

In the hospital wards, you hear this sad cry
From the wounded, sick and those near to die.
Midst the stench of the casts, the cries of the sick
Would pierce, you'd imagine, a man to the quick,
But what addled-eared bastards will coolly ignore?
Not the Q.M.C., but the Medical Corps.

While the troops were existing on salmon and rice,
Some HQ's were living on meat, milk, and ice,
Cereals, hot cakes, eggs, bacon and fruit,
Ham and tomatoes, the share of the loot
Which could be obtained through friendship, or quicker,
You may not believe it; a good shot of liquor.
Who sent to "The Rock" all our rations, type E?
Not the Medical Corps, but the Q.M.C.

Then, after surrender, with the death rate increasing
From malaria, dysentery, and the effects of poor eating,
When lives might be saved by prompt application
Of existing supplies of the right medication,
Who was it retained at high prices, the drugs
That might have brought health to score upon score?
Not the Q.M.C., but the Medical Corps.

"... In fact, I hate this whole damn' life ..."

Prison Camp Eulogy and Addenda

There are things about a prison camp
That I don't like: no bedside lamps
For reading nights, the lack of books,
The rough and overbearing cooks,
No privacy, no private places,
The close-cropped heads and hairy faces,
The tasty food that's never here,
The dysentery and diarrhea,
The habit of calling pesos "P's,"
The absence of mango trees,
The acrid smoke of galley fires,
The all-enclosing Jap barbed wire,
The loud and almost ceaseless chatter
Of little men who do not matter,
The maggots, flies, and dripping rain,
The sale of medicines for gain,
Some heroes of Corregidor
Whose bravery grows more and more
With every time they glibly tell
Of how they spurned each bomb and shell,
Of rumors that were daily rife,
In fact, I hate this whole damn' life—
Our chow deluxe, or sardines tinned,
The smell that comes with each west wind,
The sniping of our cigarette butts,
The dirty gutters 'round the huts,
The athlete's foot, or scurvied mouth,
That pretty phrase, "You God-damned louse."

For months we've fed on rice and greens
With, now and then, some mungo beans,
And dreamed of meals at Jai-Alai,*
And all the food that cash can buy.
For months we've slept on ground or floor
And wake each morning, stiff and sore.
At night we rise six times, or eight,
To have to run and urinate.
For months we've had no news but scuttle
Or Japoganda most unsubtle.
We don't know if the Yanks are landing,
Or if our captors are disbanding.

For months we've listened to army slang,
Fouler than the jargon of an east side gang;
Been ordered round by an upper ranker
With an IQ minus, or even blanker,
But it won't be long now, it can't be long now,
Before we never again see lugao,†
Or have to supplement our chow
With purchases from army truckers—
The lousy, profiteering suckers—
Before we sleep in cozy nests
Of eiderdown or beauty rest
Within a room that's warm and clean,
Away from dirt and bum latrines,
Before we quit this bloody hole,
And drink a hole in our payroll,

---

* This was a very nice building in Manila before the war where the game of jai-alai was played. I was never inside the building, but I was told it was very nice and there was a good restaurant in it.
† A term we used for rice boiled in water and stirred while cooking to make a sort of gruel.

And look once more the well-dressed mister,
And not an animated blister,
Before we'll never want for rain
To wash away the dirt and stain
Of sweat and mud and sticky clay
Accumulated day by day,
And lose the red-eyed, blue-backed flies
That foul our annual chocolate rice,
And get relief from rain and heat,
And use a normal toilet seat.
We'll soon stop this sort of thing
As guests of Nippon's Sun God King.
No longer we'll salute and bow;
The Yanks will soon be in Mindanao.
Guerrillas roam the countryside
Unless our very ears have lied.
In thirty days, or some weeks more,
We'll be the guests of Ecuador.*
Or spreading it a little thinly,
We'll leave forthwith for Fort McKinley.
God knows we soon must leave this army
Before we go completely balmy;
Maddened by the pricks divinal
Of some tunnel-squatting colonel.
Soon we'll leave this Bongabon;
It won't be long, it won't be long.

---

* This refers to a rumor that was rampant at one time to the effect that Japan and the U.S. had reached an agreement to exchange prisoners of war on the condition that they be sent to a neutral country for the duration of the war. The rumor had it that Ecuador had agreed to accept custody of the American prisoners.

Addenda

Oh friend, your plaintive late lament
Has reached a sympathetic ear,
And brought to life the urge to vent
A few more deprecations here.
It irks me sore to be addressed
By "Nippers" as "The Emperor's Guest,"
And directed here and there by grunts
Of bandy-legged little runts.
I'm sick of rice, tasteless and flat,
With foreign bits of this and that
Contributing to contamination
That won't invite examination;
Of campaign hats worn cowboy fashion;
Tired of soggy, muddy boots,
Of hillbillies dressed in soldier suits,
Of groping in the dark at night,
Of getting up before it's light
To face a barren, empty day;
Of trying to fill it in some way
With idle, futile, useless choring,
Cares or pastimes just as boring;
Adorning mess kits, for example,
This lousy poetry is a sample.
I'm tired of going without meat,
Of sitting on a still-warm seat,
Of flies that hatch from maggots there,
And soar and buzz 'round bottoms bare,
Of seeing sores on hands and legs,
Of shaven pates as bald as eggs;

Tired of someone's tuneless whistle,
Of wild-haired beards that droop or bristle,
Of itching back or raw-rubbed hips
Scratched by roughened bamboo strips;
Tired of childish, loud discussions;
Tired of rectal repercussions,
Malodorous, oleaginous ones,
Resounding through the night like guns.
I'm tired of hearing men called "Joe",
Of dividing things just so and so,
Of splitting seven spoons of stew,
One for me and one for you,
Of endless lines on every hand,
Where eternally I'm forced to stand
At muster, chow, early or late,
Even when I defecate.
Everything I want to do,
A thousand others want it, too.
Fed up with the constant blowing
Of the hero crop that's daily growing;
Who speak of tunnel rats as "they",
When "we" is what they ought to say.
Tired of weird yardbird gyrations,
Of officer's puerile machinations,
To look out for number one,
And devil take the hindmost one;
Of an army that seems to think "civilians"
Is a term synonymous with "millions".
Tired of rumors varied and diverse
Peddled by drivers well-rehearsed,
Of scuttle-butt without surcease,
Or speculations on release.

Sick of trying to solve the riddle
Of getting up at nights to piddle.
Tired of the muddy trails we tread,
Of nocturnal visits to the "head",
Of seeing hope and dreams at night
Come crashing down in morning light.
To this miserable existence,
In fact I'm losing my resistance.
I'm tired of the motley multitude
That daily I must see,
And if you ask one of them,
You'll find they're just as tired of me.

Fall and Disgrace of Old Glory

You all know the grim story,
But there are those who didn't see
The fall and disgrace of "Old Glory"
And what it meant to me.

Probably by now we're forgotten
By those who sent us to die
In the unprepared islands begotten
By Dewey, so noble and sly.

Our country, you know, has billions
In food and silver and gold;
Personnel and materials in millions,
Why, buddy, the half can't be told!

Yes, we know she'll not be beaten.
Proud and free she'll always stand.
And although her pride we have eaten,
On her shores we still long to stand.

But I wonder what our folks will think
When we tell them, by and by,
How we fought in the heat, rain and stink,
Only to be captured, to starve and die.

Months of jungle fighting
With enemy planes overhead;
Malaria mosquitoes biting
Amidst the whistle and whine of lead.

Sleepless nights of waiting
For help that never came;
Nerves so tense and grating;
Bleeding and sore, and lame.

Prayers and tears for our loved ones
So far away from home.
Tears for our buddies who died and bled
From cuts, bruises and mangled bones.

Dreaming of homes and loved ones
Ten thousand miles away;
Listening to the roar of the big guns
At the dawn of every day.

Does anyone dare call you a coward
Because you broke and ran
When at last we were overpowered,
And surrendered Corregidor and Bataan?

They may think that is where it all ended,
And from there on it was fun,
But when in the prisons the Japs founded,
The fight had just begun.

Thrown into mud-bound prison camps
To live with rats, fleas, and lice;
To suffer and die from disease and cramps
From eating weeds and wormy rice.

What has happened to the starry flag
Which o'er the islands was flown?

It now adorns a Jap sleeping bag,
And on the ground each night is thrown.

They replaced it with the flaming red sun;
The symbol of Japan,
But they can't replace the sore we feel
For Old Glory, Corregidor and Bataan.*

---

* After the surrender of Corregidor, most of the American survivors were sent to Cabanatuan Prison Camp No. 3. There was a road through the camp separating the Japanese side—where the guards were quartered—from the American side. One of the Japanese guards had captured a large American flag. He used it to wrap his bedroll in. It appeared to us that he made every effort to desecrate our flag by displaying it before us in every vulgar way he could think of. For example, I have seen him spread it on the ground and lay his blankets over it, drape it over a barbed wire fence and drag it on the ground. This is what the writer of the poem above was referring to.

They Know You

They can't fool me, you're a soldier
That saw duty in the fight for Bataan.
The public can easily identify you
For you still cook "Quan" in the can.
Just because you quit wearing khaki,
Or carrying a rifle on your shoulder;
We know you for one of the forgotten;
You're still shooting butts in a holder.
And buddy, those tricks of eating
(That would quick make Emily Post swoon)
Mark you for one of the battlers
Who ate everything out of a spoon.
The fact that you hide salt and sugar
Doesn't disguise you either, man,
And only a Cabanatuan prisoner
Would scrape the inside of a can.
Maybe that duck-walking shuffle
Peculiar to the beri-beri group
Wouldn't be quite so noticable
If instead of squatting, you'd stoop.
But brother, you might have escaped
Being recognized by all of the horde
By using a few simple ruses,
If Henry hadn't given you a Ford.[*]

— Frank A. Majors

[*] This refers to the rumor that got started that Henry Ford had pledged to give each American survivor of the defense of the Philippines a new Ford after the war.

Unsung Heroes

As I lie here in the twilight
And the day is nearly done,
I cannot help but ponder
As I watch the setting sun,
About the pals who are gone forever
Who were taken in their prime,
Not by bullets or bombings,
But by age old Father Time.

Though I blame their fatal passing
On the wily Japanese,
It is entered in the record
As a tropical disease.
"Beri-beri" was the comment
As they buried several score.
Dysentery and malaria both
Claimed their share and more.

We were dying by the thousands
With no relief in sight;
It was there the U.S. Army
Faced its very toughest fight.
Yes, the heroes were in plenty
On the mountains of Bataan,
But the ones we're now producing
Make them look like "also ran."

Day by day they faced the struggle;
It continues through the night,

And their battle cry like Butler's
Is, "We've just begun to fight."
Just whom am I defending
As the heroes of this game?
Who are all the brave contenders
For the halls of mortal fame?

There's no array of medals
To decorate their breasts;
Just an armband with a red cross,
But it sure has stood the test.
For the most the war was over
When each man gave up his gun,
But for them the war was starting
With a fight from sun to sun.

Yes, the heroes who have battled,
Never ceasing, in their fight
From the early rays of morning
To the dawn of early light,
Are the "medics", never ceasing
As they face each new-born day,
Fight to save another soldier
Who had fallen by the way.

There is far, far greater danger
Than the battles of the war,
For they daily face the danger
Of disease's fatal scar.
They are heroes, don't forget,
Though not mentioned by the pen,
And their fight continues daily
Just to save the lives of men.

No medals theirs, with papers
To give credence to the story
How they slew by thousands, men,
For war's eternal glory.
No, the payment they are given
As they face the setting sun,
Is the knowledge that they face it
With a job that's been well done.

— S/Sgt. Samuel E. Poole

Intermission

Today I feel like a man anew
This, truthfully, I say;
I left this atmosphere of blue
And saw the boys across the way.

I cannot tell or quite express
The feelings deep within,
Of how my heart would jump, no less,
When each would smile or grin.

I could see a future in each face,
And hope in every smile,
A carefree laugh that held in place
The things in life worthwhile.

They talked not of pity or of pain
Or how long it would be
Before we'd live like men again
And freedom once more see.

We recalled the happenings of yesterday;
The combat of men and steel,
The fight to exist along the way,
The struggle from meal to meal.

We talked in terms of schoolboys, yet—
Of the days that could not last.
We laughed and talked as to forget
The horrors of the past.

And over here, within these gates,
With all the ills and trials,
A sick and brooding man debates
His power, strengths and fears.

He asks and begs for all who care
To give a helping hand
And feel the duty there to share
Until he alone can stand.

He has his future that he plans
That on all life depends,
His living there from day to day
With hopes that have no end.

But some have lost the gift of dreams,
And to themselves denied
The beauty of the future that brightly beams,
The past to view with pride.

— Elmer Smith
Feb. 28, 1943

Scuttlebutts

When our children read in history
Of MacArthur's little band,
Little will they know the mystery
That caused our vital stand.

I think now that the thing
That gave us those iron-clad guts,
Was the stories that in our heads did ring—
Better known as "scuttlebutts".

The sky tomorrow will be black with planes
Our captain told us on the wire.
They'll be friendly planes from Australia's lanes,
So be sure before you fire.

That night as we cleaned and oiled our guns,
Our spirits soared on high.
We never dreamed that just for fun
Our B.C. would tell a lie.

The next morning, sure enough they came,
A hundred planes or more,
But they had red spots upon each wing,
The same as we'd seen before.

Well, that was rumor number one,
And we just banged away,
And fed the shells to our hungry guns;
The same as every day.

Now a friend of a friend of a pal of mine,
So the stories always go,
Just told me one hot off the line
'Cause a colonel said it was so.

The Yanks and tanks are coming;
In fact, they're almost here,
But you mustn't let this get running;
It's strictly confidential, you hear.

Talk about old maids in black bloomers
As she gossips and the flapper ramps,
She could never keep up with the rumors
In Cabanatuan Prison Camps.

When at last it's all over,
And we leave the nipa huts,
We'll sail for the land of clover
With the latest "scuttlebutts."

Heroes Modern

With bated breath and awe-struck ear,
We heard the sentence loud and clear.
"Ten men must die," we heard him say,
And we stood unbelieving that fateful day.

The ten, they knew that they must die,
Although, for truth, they knew not why.
Their lives had run their brief, short spans.
They were paying the price of another man.

We saw them die that sorrowful day.
Little solace, they died the American way.
Hearts for them, at home will bleed.
For the price they paid, there was no need.

Of old heroes I've heard and read,
But these ten men who now are dead;
We salute them one; we salute them all.
Ten finer heroes never did fall.

As o'er your resting place, sod does form,
A spot in our hearts for you stays warm.
For we who knew you in the past
Know now full well, your glory shall last.*

---

* The above poem was written by someone who had witnessed the execution of ten men because one in the group had escaped. This probably happened in the first months of our captivity. Later, in the established prison camps, we were divided into ten-man squads. We were informed by the Japs that if any member of a squad escaped, the other nine men would be executed. There were several cases where this was actually carried out. The reason I assume the case referred to in the poem was

In a Hurry

There was a line at the latrine
At least a hundred strong.
Every rank and degree of service
Composed the motley throng.
It was a time of dire distress;
A period of greatest urgency.
Preference was frequently given
To those of greatest emergency.
No thoughts of rank were entertained
It really was man to man;
All was common sense and decency
And not the army plan.
The file was rudely broken;
All order completely gone
With a cry, "Make room for the colonel,
He feels a movement coming on."
When up strode the mighty man;
He towered five foot three.
His mighty calves were quartered;
He wore breeches to the knee.
His cheeks were apple rosy,
And his belly was so round
That it was clear to everyone
He'd done his fighting underground.
But he'd certainly broke that line
And caused a great amount of grief;

---

early in our captivity is that ten were executed instead of nine, meaning we had not
been divided into ten-man squads.

Such is the power heeded
To that sacred silver leaf.
He pushed right to the center,
And no one did resist
Until he met an old time sergeant
Who turned around and hissed,
"Sir, I've studied the Articles of War
And every regulation,
But I fail to find a paragraph
That covers defecation."
The colonel fumed and ranted,
But finally broke down and pled.
But the sergeant held his ground
Like a soldier born and bred.
He said, "For twenty years I've taken dirt
From just the likes of you,
And though you bust me back to private,
I'll see this thing through."
The colonel then was silent,
And the line continued on its round.
But next day the colonel's washing
Was stained a lovely brown.

— Lt. Keith Madell

Prison Camp Number Three

We're out on the edge of nowhere
Ringed 'round with a cordon of steel.
We've been hammered and numbed 'til some of us
Have forgotten how to feel.

We've forgotten the clasp of friendly hands,
And the love for the arts that are true;
We've forgotten to laugh, and some of us
Have forgotten the friends that we knew.

But "dog eat dog" and "to hell with you"
Do not, and never will, rhyme
With brotherly love and truth and God
And the cards at Christmas time.

Let's remember the tints of autumn leaves
And the beauty of drifted snow.
Let's remember the smiles and the songs we sang
In the warmth of the campfire's glow.

Let's remember the folks back home
And the sweethearts who wait and pray
That the same swell guy who left them
Will be coming back some day.

Forgotten Men of Bataan

In a camp of nipa barracks
Lost deep in the Philippines,
There's a group of American soldiers
With nothing left but dreams.

They are fighting a greater battle
Than the one they fought and lost.
It's a battle against the elements;
A battle with life at cost.

Some came through the awful torture
Like days and nights in hell,
In the struggles for that little "ride" *
Where many a brave man fell.

But now it's not what you know
Or how quick you bite the dirt;
It's not the hate you once held
Or whether you're poor or rich.

No one cares who you were back home,
Or what kind of life you led,

---

* I have been asked to explain this phrase. Since I did not write the poem, I cannot be sure, but I take it to mean the Bataan Death March. The march was from Mariveles on the southern tip of Bataan to the town of San Fernando, a distance of approximately 55 miles. The prisoners were loaded into boxcars at San Fernando and shipped to Capas, from where they marched to Camp O'Donnell, where thousands more died. I believe the little "ride" refers to that ride in the cramped, stuffy boxcars from San Fernando to Capas, which is approximately 30 miles.

It's just how long you can stick it out
That governs your life instead.

The battle we're fighting at present
Against mosquitoes, flies, and disease;
With decent living conditions,
We could fight our case with ease.

It's rice for morning, noon and night;
It rains 'most every day,
And we sleep on nothing but bamboo slats
We've no better place to lay.

We eat from any old tin plate
That we may be able to get;
We're the forgotten men of Bataan
fighting the hardest fight yet.

Those of us who do come through
Perhaps can praise our worth,
And tell a very strange tale
Of a terrible "Hell on Earth."

A Ghost Passes By

Once these islands were alive and gay;
Youth was in blossom out this way.
Ladies were here with an added zest;
Good times we had, some of the best.
We now dream, to wake up with a sigh,
For now they are ghosts, passing us by.

The women are gone; the men now long
For their beauty, their laughter and song.
Drunks, we had hoped we'd forget;
Not the happy memories of folks we'd met.
The happy-go-lucky, the brave, and the strong
Are now ghosts, treading along.

War has destroyed this beautiful isle;
You'll never again see a native smile.
Dancing and laughter have ceased to be
'Til America comes from across the sea.
While we wait in the prison camp;
While in review these ghosts do tramp.

On evenings in an increasing line,
Slowly they walk, your pals and mine.
As you are, I once was, and as I am, you will be;
It is foolish to live; give up and come with me.
Join us, brothers, we are your friends;
We are now ghosts, but once we were men.

We fought, and were their sole defenders
Until these isles did surrender.
In prison camp, so hard we tried
To keep alive, but many died.
It was easier to forget it all
And join the ghosts when they did call.

God have mercy and hear my prayer;
Must I live forever in despair?
Give me the courage to say "no"
When the ghosts beckon for me to go.
Give thanks to God, all who have not died;
To create a will to live and understand
That we'll soon go home to America's land.

The Call of War

Send me your youth, the best of your youth,
The courageous, clean, and strong,
From city, hamlet, and countryside,
Where life is a careless song.
Have him forget his house of dreams,
With ivy 'round his door.
I have a job for his eager feet;
Wallowing deep in gore.

Send me your youth, the pick of your youth,
You can keep the other kind.
I'll tear the smile from his careless lips,
The dreams from his boyish mind.
I'll send him where the cannon roar
And rend him limb from limb,
And when I'm through, you can have him back;
Or all that's left of him.

In a mind that is free from brutality,
I'll sow the seeds of hate
'Til he rushes forth with a lust to kill
Like a crazed inebriate.
I'll twist his soul with shameful lies
As he carries my banners high,
And prate to him of a noble cause
As he stumbles out to die.

You've sent me your youth, the best of your youth,
A thousand times or more.

I've left their bones in a shallow grave
On some beleaguered shore.
I've plundered the world and laid it waste
With youth as my helpless tools.
Each time I call, you send them all;
For you are such hopeless fools.

— Martin F. Owens

"... laughing boys
fought and died"

Sleep in Peace

Sleep in peace, ye men of Flanders;
Your sons too befell the fate
Into which you were led;
While millions cheered their heroes dead
Far home across the sea, too late.

We, too, ye men of Flanders field,
In youth, left all who shared
Our sorrows, tears, and joys.
We, too, as a group of laughing boys
Fought and died for those who cared.

Sleep in peace; rest eternally.
The larks still sing their song.
The fiery torch you nobly gave
Is not with us in our dark grave,
But with our sons to carry on.

— Elmer Smith

I Wonder

I sometimes wonder if my dreams
Of home will all come true,
And if the nightmare of these days
Will vanish in the blue.
I wonder when the Yanks will come,
And when the Japanese will run.
I wonder if the folks at home are having any fun.
I wonder just how long we'll wait.
We won't be here forever.
Perhaps quite soon our luck will change,
And we'll be free—I wonder.

Requiem

God rest ye dead and rest ye well,
'Tis blest ye be, freed from this hell.
Though unmarked be thy grave with cross and flower,
Dims not the glory of thine hour.

Let not thy loved ones for thee mourn,
For men with thy spirit will again be born.
Men with hearts as brave as thine
From whose hands the torch of peace shall shine.

The Flag Speaks

I am your flag, a symbol of life.
With stars and stripes that gleam;
Serving in struggle, panic, and strife;
What e'er be your pleasure, reason, or dream.

I am your power, your own strength and will.
Serving those who follow or valiantly guide.
I am the battlefield, ocean foam, and will.
I am the soldier or pilot who died.

I am the blood that heroes and martyrs shed,
Who fought and died my stripes to save.
I am each bomb, each salvo of lead;
I am the tears that follow each one to his grave.

I am a mystery, men know not why.
I am their belief, they cannot see.
The soldier, the men who valiantly try;
I am all they believed I can be.

— Elmer Smith
October, 1942

The American Way

What does life hold for you, man?
What do you crave and desire?
What strength binds you to a barbarous land?
A few fixed guns and wire.
What lies behind your eagerness strong?
What makes you think life worthwhile?
Now that your buddies and friends are gone,
How can you take life with a smile?

How can you toil from morn 'til night
In rain and the burning sun?
How can you control your emotions and might
When your guard has but bayonet and gun?
Why do you do it? What is your aim?
Do you have a goal or a price?
It's not for glory or fortune or fame;
Surely not your ration of rice.

You're not contented, that has been seen
In your compound of barbed wire high,
But you still love to see a sunset serene
Against an oriental sky.
You stand your bango at six and eight
To be counted like cattle and sheep.
A hard wooden floor you appreciate
When you're allowed to rest or sleep.

You must have a reason for such courage and will
To live above shame and disgrace,

Kneeling to stupidity and still
Carry a smile on your face.
I know you've a secret, for every man
Has dreams and hope for tomorrow.
Is your dream of love, or a lurid plan
To avenge your brother's sorrow?

Do you plan revenge on a battlefield,
With hatred aflame in your breast;
Sown by the whine of deadly steel;
Matured by moral unrest?
Do you plan to repay the same way
All the heartache, humiliation, and pain,
And death of those of yesterday,
And the torture of those who remain?

Or do you intend to act as a friend
And observe God's Golden Rule;
Replacing the hate as your ties will mend
With friendliness as your tool?
But remember, young man, this had its test;
A great man once said in retreat,
"East is east and west is west
And ne'er the twain shall meet."

Or do you toil for the day you'll see
Your homeland shores that wait
Under the spreading arm of Liberty
Or the crest of the Golden Gate?
Is it that which awaits you, your price and goal
That accounts beyond bravery;
Submitting to hands that cruelly stole
Your body to slavery?

Or if you have a reason, let's hear it,
And begin at the very start.
You had the seed of American Spirit
Embedded deep in your heart.
You've not one reason alone, young man,
That you can honestly say
To be exact, no other than,
"I was taught the American Way."

— Elmer Smith
Oct. 11, 1943

Beneath the Lights of Home

I can see the lights of home
Shining brightly o'er the foam;
Beckon to me while I roam
Away from the lights of home.

In that little old sleepy town,
Nothing happens after the sun goes down.
Nothing but moonbeams roam around
Beneath the lights of home.

Turn the hands of time for me;
Let me live in my memory.
Once again I long to be
Beneath the lights of home.

"... and sing to Thee eternal praise"

Prisoner's Prayer

Oh Lord of all, who reigns on high,
I see thy works up in the sky,
The brilliant gold of every dawn,
The sunset's beauties finely drawn,
And see at times thy pure rainbow,
A promise true to us below.

I lift my eyes up to the hills,
And like the psalmist, my heart fills
With strength to carry on the fight
To live for freedom and the right.
My thanks, Oh Lord, for all you made,
And thy rich grace that gives me aid.

For what we have, we give our thanks,
Those riches never found in banks.
For shelter, clothing, and our food,
No matter if it may be crude,
But most I thank thee for the peace
That brings to our frail hearts surcease.

How long, oh Lord of all that's just,
Must we as prisoners in here rust?
We are beneath the enemy,
But give us strength and power to see
Beyond this military jail
When we're delivered from travail.

And through the years on out ahead
My gratitude will not go dead,
But rather, I will keep in mind
The blessings of most every kind,
Recall this mercy in these days
And sing to Thee eternal praise. Amen.

Look Up

When the going gets too rough, Bud,
And your feet ache day and night;
When your stomach cramps and fever burns
'Til you've lost the will to fight;
Don't think then, Bud, of quitting;
You only need look up.

Look up to where the stars shine
And the moon wings through the sky,
And from your heart send forth a call
To him that reigns on high.
You haven't been alone, Bud;
You only need to ask.
A single word sent from the heart
Will send him to the task.

God made the seas and the verdant hills;
The stars that light the sky
And creeping things, the beasts and flowers
And all the birds that fly.
The making of each grain of sand
Was not too small to do.
Then don't think that God above
Has now forgotten you.

So when the pain is torment,
And life's a bitter cup,
His help is waiting, Bud, for you;
You only need look up.

Dealer of Fate

Oh dealer, hear us calling;
We do not know your name,
Or that you do exist
Except we've known your fame.
Anxiously we are waiting
For our release from shame.

Month on month its been
That you double ruled our fate.
Your ugly duckling brother
Who delightedly made us wait
Our long-sought liberation
'Til some far distant date.

Again we are seeking
Your friendly, smiling face
That bids us to be patient
While miracles take place,
And hope that you're preparing
A happy ending in our case.

We know that you've been busy
With your friend over there.
Perhaps it's to our advantage
To have to wait and share
The victorious consummation
That will redeem their fare.

Anyhow, we've been thinking;
Who did forget we've earned
With heroic determination
A peace no man would spurn,
And merit soon the freedom
For which so long we've yearned.

Yes, dealer, we are waiting.
It's our turn to win the pot.
Luck can't always be against us
Although we're on the spot.
So deal us soon a better hand
And we'll back it with all we've got.

— Frank A. Majors

Prison Impressions

Within the great gates of a prison camp,
The world seems void of love,
But should one's eyes upward stray,
They behold God's blue world above.

The days seem endless within the camp;
Your spirits rise and fall,
But give one thought to God above;
These vanish one and all.

Should doubt of release assail you
Within these prison gates,
Think of God's wide world above
And the rewards for those who wait.

The following poem was not written in prison camp nor was it written by a prisoner. It was written by a high-school girl during World War II and she was 15 years old at the time. The poem was inspired by a picture of a group of prisoners of war which appeared in an issue of *Life* magazine during the war. I am including it because I think it shows extraordinary insight for a girl of that age and, by strange coincidence, that girl is now my dear wife. We didn't meet until about six years after the war was over. She was reared in Ohio and I was reared in Texas. We met when we were both attending The University of Texas.

Prisoner of War

Now on the pictured page, he comes to life—
The terror-stricken brother of all men,
Brother of all, rejected by full half the world.
Will he go back again?

Back to the home and ways he knew and loved,
Back to the wide skies of his native land?
Can those who hold him captive realize
The home-sickness in this mute prisoner band?

His anguished eyes look at his foes in pain.
Young he is, heart-bewildered and alone.
He is their brother, whom they say they hate,
But when he asks for bread, will they give stone?

The roar of battle no more pounds his ears.
He will, in time, forget his seething fright;
But sometimes, perhaps, like a little child,
He will awake in panic in the night.

— Beverly Biery

Songs

Battle Hymn of Bataan

Dugout Doug MacArthur lies shaking in "The Rock,"
Safe from all the bombers and any sudden shock.
Dugout Doug is eating from the best there is in stock,
And his troops go starving on.

Chorus:
Dugout Doug, come out of hiding.
Dugout Doug, come out of hiding.
Send to Frankie the glad tidings
That his troops go starving on.

Dugout Doug's not timid; he's just cautious, not afraid.
He's protecting carefully the stars that Frankie made.
Four star generals are as rare as sugar on Bataan,
And his troops go starving on.
Chorus

Dugout Doug is ready in his Chris-Craft for to flee
O'er the bouncing billows and the wildly raging sea;
For the Japanese are pounding at the gates of old Bataan,
And his troops go starving on.
Chorus

We have fought this war the hard way since they said
        the fight was on,
All the way from Lingayen to the hills of old Bataan,
And we'll continue fighting when old Dugout Doug is
        gone
And still go starving on.

Chorus:
Dugout Doug came out of hiding.
Dugout Doug came out of hiding.
On a submarine you must go riding
While your troops go starving on.

Iron Horse Battalion

Gay we ride over rocks and ruts;
We got what it takes—just plenty of guts.
The driver's drunk; the commander's nuts,
In the Iron Horse Battalion.

Our colors are scarlet, yellow and blue;
We take them Christian, heathen, or Jew.
If you're a screw-up, they'll sign you, too,
In the Iron Horse Battalion.

You've always got to wear a grin,
Tanked on whiskey, beer, or gin,
But be sure to cut your lovie in,
In the Iron Horse Battalion.

Like the boys in the cavalry;
The gold bricks of the infantry,
We got sore feet, but proud to be
In the Iron Horse Battalion.

The private gets just what he makes.
He does his part and shares the breaks.
He does no work, but his ass sure aches
In the Iron Horse Battalion.

The corporal here is just the same;
He catches hell and all the blame;
No respect for such a name
In the Iron Horse Battalion.

The sergeant buck has to fulfill
A job that sends him o'er the hill;
Recruits that never heard of drill
In the Iron Horse Battalion.

You might think we had a snap,
But it's all work, and that's no crap;
Playing nursemaid to a pile of scrap
In the Iron Horse Battalion.

A hundred and fifty times I swore
I'd sign up in the Medical Corps,
But I always just came back for more
In the Iron Horse Battalion.

— Elmer Smith[*]

---

[*] Elmer Smith was in a tank battalion. The above poem was intended to be sung to the tune of "Here We Go 'Round the Mulberry Bush."

Thanks for the Memories

Thanks for the memories
Of shells and bombs and such,
And chow that wasn't much;
The sinking of our navy
With the British and the Dutch.
How lousy it was.

Thanks for the memories
Of bombs on Corregidor;
The fall of Singapore;
The runout of MacArthur
On the submarine D-4.
How lousy it was.

Seldom's the time that we feasted,
And many's the time that we fasted.
Oh, it was hell while it lasted.
We had fun, and we did run.

Oh thanks for the memories
Of rumors, although new,
They never did come true,
So it's the Golden Gate by '48,
And I guess it will have to do;
Oh, thank you so much.

The following song was written by a group of Australian officers in the prison camp I was in when the war ended. The camp was located in the northern part of Honshu in Japan. It was written immediately after we were informed of the surrender of Japan, and a group of officers sang the song at a camp gathering that night. The song is sung to the tune of an old British Army ballad called "Troop Ship."

Soldier's (Prisoner's) Farewell

There's a troop ship that's leaving next week
Bound for we don't know where,
But as long as it takes us away from Japan
We none of us bloody well care.
Just think of the millions we are leaving behind,
The bastards that have to live here.
We leave them their rice and their fleas and their lice,
And we leave them goodbye with a cheer.

Chorus:
Bless them all; bless them all,
The long and the short and the tall.
Bless all the one-stars and bless all the twos;
Bless all the "Honchoes" and bless all the fools,
For we are saying goodbye to them all
As back to their "benjoes" they crawl.[*]
Next week, we've a notion, we'll be on the ocean,
So cheer up, me lads, bless them all.

Nipponese don't worry me; Nipponese don't worry me;
Let them "Kiotski";
Let them "Kuda";
It's not going to hurt in the place where we are,

---

[*] This phrase refers to the fact that the Japanese in rural areas carried the excrement from the toilets (benjoes) and spread it in their fields or gardens for fertilizer. They carried it in buckets suspended from each end of a yoke across their shoulders. We referred to the yoke as a "yo-yo pole" and to the buckets as "honey buckets." The song implies that the Japanese guards will be going back to work on farms and that this task will be part of their duties.

And we're saying goodbye to them all
As back to their "benjoes" they crawl.
Next week, we've a notion, we'll be on the ocean,
So cheer up, me lads, bless them all.

News Comments
on the Fall of Bataan

News Comments
on the Fall of Bataan
(Quoted from news sheet published on Corregidor, April 16, 1942.)

It makes one feel proud.

— Roosevelt

The Bataan forces went out as they would have wished; fighting to the end of their flickering, forlorn hope. No army has ever done so much with so little, and nothing became it more than its last trial and agony. To the ever-praying mothers of its dead, I can only say that the halo of Jesus of Nazareth has descended upon their souls and that God will take them unto himself.

— MacArthur

Tonight we must end on a note of sorrowful pride. Britain has been moved. The four months defense of Bataan is ended. They have written a story that will never be forgotten.

— London Radio

Bataan has fallen, but the spirit that made it stand a beacon to all liberty-loving people of the world, can not fail.

— Voice of Freedom*

---

* The "Voice of Freedom" station quoted in "News Comments on Bataan" was the Voice of Freedom radio station on Corregidor. This station was set up after the fall of Manila. It identified itself only as "the Voice of Freedom, broadcasting from somewhere in the Philippines." This quotation is the last sentence of the broadcast announcing the fall of Bataan. The complete text of the announcement appears following the quotations from the Corregidor news sheet.

I have nothing but praise for the men who conducted this epic battle. Our troops, outnumbered, worn down by constant fighting, and exhausted by insufficient rations and disease, have had their lines broken down. A long and gallant defense has been overthrown.

— Secretary Stimson

No defeat can ever dim the glory of the Bataan defenders. No reverse will ever lower our pride in lifting them to the ranks of America's greatest heroes. America's regard for them is an emotion too real and personal to parade. Bataan will be a symbol of those who fought without fear.

— *Washington, D.C. News*

Our debt to the men of Bataan must be paid. It must be the mightiest devotion and upsurge of energy of men and women in the nation.

— *Dakota Tribune*

The war was not won or lost on Bataan. Bataan's was a bugle call to the attack. Bataan has told us how to win the war.

— *San Francisco Chronicle*

Tributes of words seem empty and inadequate. It is enough merely to say that the Bataan defenders will be immortal.

— *St. Louis Globe-Democrat*

To the weary men who have at last been defeated by superior forces on Bataan, the praise of their countrymen brings cold comfort. They would have preferred to fight the Japanese on something like equal terms. The chance was denied them. We know from what Stimson has told us, that a few successful efforts were made to supply them through the Japanese blockade, and thanks to those efforts, the men were never short on ammunition, but this and pluck were all they had. They lacked guns and heavy air support. Their delaying action performed with gallantry will take their place forever in the traditions of America. Bataan has been lost, but it will be remembered generations from now.

— *New York Times*

The men of Bataan have given the world a wonderful legacy. In gratitude to these wonderful men, we must close our ranks and do our duty.

The following is the full text of the April 10, 1942 Voice of Freedom broadcast announcing the fall of Bataan:

"BATAAN HAS FALLEN. The Philippine-American troops on this war-ravaged and blood-stained peninsula have laid down their arms. With heads bloody yet unbowed, they have yielded to superior force and numbers of the enemy.

"The world will long remember the epic struggle that Filipino and American soldiers put up in these jungle fastnesses and along the rugged coast of Bataan.

"They have stood uncomplaining under the constant and grueling fire of the enemy for more than three months. Besieged on land and blockaded by sea, cut off from all sources of help in the Philippines and in America, these intrepid fighters have done all that human endurance could bear.

"For what sustained them through all these months of incessant battle was a force that was more than merely physical. It was the force of an unconquerable faith—something in the heart and soul that physical hardship and adversity could not destroy! It was the thought of native land and all that it holds most dear, the thought of freedom and dignity, the pride in these most priceless of all human prerogatives.

"The adversary, in the pride of his power and triumph, will credit our troops with nothing less than the courage and fortitude that his own troops have shown. All the world will testify to the almost superhuman endurance with which they stood up until the last in the face of overwhelming odds.

"But the decision had to come. Men fighting under the banner of unshakeable faith are made of something more than flesh, but they are not made of impervious steel. The flesh must yield at last, endurance melts away, and the end of the battle must come.

"Bataan has fallen, but the spirit that made it stand—a beacon to all the liberty-loving peoples of the world—cannot fail." [*]

---

[*] This was written by Salvatore P. Lopez and read by Norman Reyes. This news broadcast from Corregidor was read again by Norman Reyes on April 8, 1967 at a shrine built on the top of Mt. Samat on Bataan, when a large group of Bataan and Corregidor veterans made a pilgrimage to the Philippines to commemorate the 25th anniversary of the fall of Bataan and Corregidor in 1942.

II

Soldiers' Pre-war Poems

Preface to Pre-War Poems

At first, I thought I would not include these pre-war poems in the same booklet with the poems written during the war because the thoughts in these poems seemed trivial and out of place when compared to the poems written during the agonies of war and Japanese prison camps. The thoughts and messages are so different.

However, after further consideration, I decided to include these poems as a separate part of the booklet. It may prove interesting for the reader to reflect upon the things which are on the minds of lonely servicemen in peace time and see the contrast with the thoughts of these men when they are suffering the tragedies of war.

I collected all of these poems while in Japanese prison camps. Judging from the subject matter, it is clear that all but three of the poems in this part were written by men on duty in the Philippines. The poem, "We've Done Our Hitch in Hell," was probably originally written in the continental United States, and several variations of it evolved as it was passed around. The poem, "A Soldier," could have been written anywhere and is applicable to about any time when we are not at war.

I first saw a copy of the poem, "Redeemed," in the prison camp in Japan where I was when the war ended. It was the last poem added to this collection except for the poem written by my wife. Judging from the content, it was written soon after the beginning of World War II. However, it must have been written before the Japanese attack on Pearl Harbor. I base this on the reasoning that, if it had been written in the U.S. after Pearl Harbor, no one in our group would have had a copy. Also, I do not believe anyone who was in the Philippines at the time of Pearl Harbor would have written this poem after the attack.

These poems give insight into the thought, concerns, and gripes of servicemen on peace-time duty in the U.S. as well as locations far from home in various places around the world.

Please reflect upon the thoughts in these poems and give the servicemen currently on duty in our armed forces the respect and consideration due them and which they deserve.

We've Done Our Hitch in Hell

I am sitting here and thinking of the things I left behind,
And I hope to put on paper what is running through my mind.
We've dug a million ditches and cleared ten miles of ground.
A meaner place this side of hell is waiting to be found,
But there's some small consolation; gather closely while I tell.
When we die we'll go to heaven for we've done our hitch in hell.

We've built a hundred kitchens for the cooks to stew our beans.
We've stood a million guard mounts, and never acted mean.
We've washed a million mess kits, and peeled a million spuds.
We've washed a million blanket rolls, and washed the captain's duds.
The number of parades we've stood is very hard to tell,
But we'll not parade in heaven for we've done our hitch in hell.

We've killed a million rats and bugs that crawled out of our eats.
We've killed a million centipedes from out our dirty sheets.
We've marched a million miles, and made a million camps.
The grub we've had to eat at times has given us the cramps.
But when our work on earth is done, our friends behind will tell,
"They surely went to heaven for they've done their hitch in hell."

When final taps is sounded, and we've laid aside life's cares,
We'll do our last parade upon those shining golden stairs.
The angels will welcome us, and harps will start to play.
We'll draw a million canteen checks, and spend them in one day.

The Great Commanding General will smile on us and say,
"Take a front seat, soldiers, you've done your hitch in hell." *

---

* In another copy of this poem, the penultimate line reads, "And this will be the word
from the Commanding General." This suits the rhyme scheme better; however, this is
given as it was written in the original manuscript as I copied it. I think this poem was
originally written in the States, but a copy made its way to the Philippines.

Thanks For the Memories

Thanks for the memories
Of nights in nipa shacks,
Rain coming through the cracks,
The bank I broke, the horse I played
On the Santa Anna track;
How lovely it was.

Thanks for the memories
On Paranaque beach,
Girls within my reach,
The Alcazar, the Metro bar,
The chaplain trying to preach,
How lovely it was.

Many a shack that I once owned,
And many the joint that I jawboned;
The tears that I shed when I sailed home,
But that's in the past; now it's just a laugh—

So thanks for the memories
Of many an all-night fling,
And Singapore gin slings.
I tried to walk, couldn't talk,
And the M.P.'s took me in
Oh thank you, so much.

The Creed of the Islands

Down in the blue China Sea
On the road to Mandalay,
Lie the spoils of Dewey's battle
In beautiful Manila Bay.

Down where there's no commandments,
And a man can raise a thirst,
Lie the outcasts and old sunshiners
The pride of Corregidor.

Down on the gin-soaked isle of Luzon,
Where the men that God forgot,
Battle malaria fever,
The dhobie itch and tropical rot.

Nobody knows they are living;
Nobody gives a damn.
Back home they were soon forgotten—
Just soldiers of Uncle Sam.

Soldiers in foreign service
Earning their meager pay;
Guarding their country's millions
For a peso twenty per day.

Living with dirty natives
Down in the Wall City zone,
Down by the Pasig River,
Ten thousand miles from home.

Sweat drenched in the evening,
They sit in the barracks and dream;
Killing their memories with liquor—
Rum, brandy, or Benedictine.

Out to Mapajo on pay day
To squander their meager pay;
To raise merry hell for an evening,
And, as usual, are broke the next day.

Back to the post for another month
God! How the time does drag;
Hardly enough filthy pesos
To supply a man with fags.

Bugs at night keep us hopping;
Mosquito bars only a lure—
Hell, no, we're not convicts—
Just soldiers on foreign tour.

A Tale of the Philippines

Before

Give me a nipa shack by the sea
With a dimpled maid to sing for me,
Pearly teeth and glossy hair,
Cool black eyes and baby stare.

Refreshing breezes from the sea,
A bouncing kidlet on my knee;
Wondrous smell of bamboo burning,
Oh nipa shack, how I am yearning.

Oh nipa shack, I'll give my stack
For you and a maid of tresses black.
You've won my heart and soul, it seems,
Oh nipa shack in the Philippines.

After

Oh nipa shack out in the sun,
A hundred dogs around me run.
A withered dame with greasy hair,
Blackened teeth, and vacant stare.

Red hot breezes from the sea,
Twelve sad-eyed kids around my knee;
Terrible stink of bamboo burning,
For lots of distance I am yearning.

Oh nipa shack, I'll give my stack
For some bamboo plates and chicken racks.
I am always broke; my clothes in pawn,
Believe me, brother, it won't be long.

Something says I've got a date
With a steamer leaving for the states.
I'm hitting for far and distant places
Among the well known open spaces.
        Adios, P. I.

It Might Be Worse

Oh boys, don't cry or bemoan your fate
With anguished moan or curse;
For there's nothing you have in the Army, boys,
That couldn't be somewhat worse.

You may think your station is awful cold,
Or deserted and devilish hot,
But it's paradise anew in comparison to
The land that God really forgot.

Yes, a land that is filthy, foul, and damp,
With bugs that bite and drone,
And the gals in town are a murky brown
With a smell that's all their own.

When you're in the mood for romance
You think of long-past dates.
You can only fret in the tropic sweat
For the women are back in the States.

And then these brown-skinned natives
Seem to turn more white
And you learn to play the tropic way—
You're a native overnight.

'Til you go to a moving picture
And see Garbo or Hedy Lamarr
Then you rave and rant for a debutante
But there aren't any where you are.

And things get even worse, boys,
And you wear a heavy frown
For it even seems the girl of your dreams
Is colored a dusky brown.

So no matter how bad your station
And in spite of this lousy verse,
Remember there's nothing you have in the Army
That the Philippines don't have worse.

The Squaw Man

Is it the heat that affects your brain
That makes you act like a man insane?
Or is it the gin you drink so free
That causes you this way to be?

To be content with a native squaw
With not a tie but common law.
Illegal children may be born
Diseased, puny, and deformed.

No chance to right the whoring birth
To show the world their real worth,
To be looked upon with sneer and slur
To be kicked around like a common cur.

Is it right to live this way?
Squaw man, you will have to pay.
You shall have to be content
When you are old and gray and bent.

And as your conscience hurts you so
With no place left to go,
All your friends have turned away
Content to let you live your way.

What in return have you to give
You who with a squaw have lived
If you should take her as your wife
Your conscience will hurt you all your life.

Pals and buddies and friends of mine
Have a life that's clean and fine.
You may ask how do I know?
I've reaped the harvest of oats I've sown.

I had a wife 'til she learned my lies
I have a daughter with her mother's eyes.
They seem to haunt me day and night
'Cause I lived a life that wasn't right.

The Curse of El Fraile

Sitting on the island of Corregidor
Am gazing toward Manila
Twenty months more, I've done four
Short timers said, "'Twas hell."

Days go by like a racing snail
With thoughts of the girl you had
Wish I could hear from her by mail
Cripes sake, I'm going mad!

Then hearing of a place called Ft. Drum
With a boat going to beaches of sand
Upon which one lies and guzzles rum
And a dark damsel holds your hand.

You transfer over with the greatest of ease
To drill upon a concrete deck
And scraping shells between your knees
You wish it would sink, by heck.

The boats don't take soldiers to lie in the sand
And get rum to quench your thirst
The maidens run at the sight of white man
That's the way El Fraile is cursed.

You rue the day the *Republic* landed
Which is much, much too late
For you are among the many stranded
And pronged by the finger of fate.

That's why you get the gloomy look
We call the "dhobie stare"
And read the pages of naughty books
And see devils everywhere.

That's why there's an empty pit
In every soldier's purse.
It went for gin to help forget
The sorry bitter curse.*

---

* El Fraile is the name of the small island in Manila Bay on which Fort Drum was built. The island was excavated to sea level and then a "concrete battleship" was built upon it. The fort was built like the forepart of a battleship. The "hull" was made of concrete 20 feet thick and about the same height. There were two 14-inch gun turrets on the top deck, and two recesses with outward-flaring walls were built into the sides for 6-inch guns. Although it was heavily shelled during the battles of both Bataan and Corregidor, it suffered no casualities at all.

A Soldier

A soldier is a nobody
We hear lots of people say
He's an outcast of the world
And always in the way.

We admit that there are bad ones
From the army to the Marines
But the majority you will find
The most worthy ever seen.

And people condemn the soldier
When he stops to take a drink or two
But does a soldier condemn you
When you stop to take a few?

Now do not scorn the soldier
But clasp him by the hand
For the uniform he wears
Means protection to your land.

The government picks its men
From the millions far and wide
So please place him as your equal
Great buddies side by side.

When a soldier goes to battle
You cheer him on his way
You say he is a hero
When in the ground he lays.

But the hardest battle of a soldier
Is in the time of peace
When all mock and scorn him
And treat him like a beast.

With these few lines we close, sir,
We hope we didn't offend
But when you meet a soldier
Just treat him as your friend.*

---

* I cannot help but wonder if this unknown poet had ever read Kipling's "Tommy."
The lot of the regular army man is apparently the same, regardless of century,
location, or name of war as recorded in history books.

The Redeemed

I saw him pass from the busy press
Of a downtown street, in his battle dress;
Swinging his arms as he walked along
Whistling the "Beer Barrel Polka" song.

With his head held high and the rhythmic beat
Of his hobnailed shoes on the busy street,
Studying his eyes and his face of tan,
I knew that our country had made a man.

I thought of his years just after school
When his only attention was dice and pool;
Then later a date with Jitterbug Jane,
Poker, and dice, and the sucker's game.

Bootleg gin and a two-bit flop;
He was gone on a road where it's hell to stop.
Where it's all downhill on a one-way track;
A damn tough grade and a long road back.

And I thought of our leaders of bygone years;
Recovery of freedom, their dreads, their fears
Of teaching boys war, denying them drill;
Claiming it gave them the lust to kill.

Our boys were denied of God, the sin
To walk in order and discipline.
So our workless lads just joined a gang
While our preachers preached and church bells rang.

And the ladies' club, I can hear them yet,
Condemning, with honor, the school cadet;
Mouthing the pacifist's tiresome prate
Of a uniform teaching our boys to hate.

But let's not forget, we're all to blame
For neglected youth and a nation's shame.
So today he's gone, and he'll never guess
How splendid he looked in his battle dress.

Swinging his arms as he walked by;
Singing his song with his head held high;
Marching to glory with his rifle and kit;
One of a million, to do his bit.

I stood up there with my shoulders straight
As he passed from sight though the station gate.
Maybe you'll come back when your battle is won;
Glory to God, my son, my son.

III

Autobiography

Bishop Davis McKendree

I was born December 28, 1919, in the small town of Vega, Texas. It is located in the Texas Panhandle approximately thirty-five miles west of Amarillo, and is the county seat of Oldham County.

My father, John William McKendree, was born October 23, 1876, in southern Kentucky, but lived in Sumner County, Tennessee, until he left to "go west" in 1901. He went first to Oklahoma, which was then known as Indian Territory. He later moved to Alanreed, Texas, where he met and married my mother, Ellen Davis, on September 15, 1908. He died August 9, 1970.

My father was named after a family member, William McKendree, who was the first native-born American to become a bishop in the Methodist Episcopal Church. The family started calling my father "Bishop" as a nickname, and that is how I came to be given "Bishop" as a first name. In later years, people began to think the name was actually a title, and as a result, I began to use my initials, B.D., rather than my first name. My family and close friends still call me "Bish."

My mother, Ellen Davis McKendree, was born in Kerr County, Texas, on October 15, 1889. Her father was a cattleman in partnership with his brother-in-law, William Hext. When my mother was a small child, the two families decided to move to Indian Territory which later became the state of Oklahoma. They drove their cattle there and ran them on the free range. I remember my mother and her older sisters telling that on the trail to Indian Territory, they were driving a herd of cattle and had several wagons to carry the women, children, and supplies. Among the supplies was a large jar of pickles. My mother was a small girl, and she could get her hand into the pickle jar, but no one else could. As a result, when they were eating a meal and someone wanted a pickle, my mother would be asked to reach in the jar and get one.

There was a story of excitement on the trail that I have heard from my mother, one of her older sisters, and from my grandmother Davis. My mother told me the part that only she could know, and the others supplied the rest of the story.

One day they were preparing to make camp for the night, and apparently all of the hands who were normally on horseback had dismounted, and most had unsaddled their horses. One of the hands was moving a wagon, which had been emptied, to its parking place for the night, and he was walking alongside. My mother ran and climbed into the wagon just for the ride, as kids will do. About that time, something spooked the team pulling the wagon, and they took off so fast that the driver dropped the reins. There they had a runaway team and wagon with my mother alone in the wagon. Uncle Bill Hext was the first one to get to his horse, and took off after them as fast as his horse could run. By this time the runaway team and wagon was over a hill and out of sight of the people in camp. My mother said she had managed to get to the tailgate of the wagon and was trying to climb out. Fortunately, the horses came to a sandy creek, which slowed them down as the wagon wheels sank in the sand, so my mother was able to jump out into the sand and was unharmed. She started walking back toward the camp when she saw her Uncle Bill come riding over the hill whipping his horse with the reins and yelling at the top of his voice. When he saw my mother trotting along, needless to say, he was quite relieved and thankful. He took her on his horse and carried her back to camp in his arms. My mother had long, black hair and as the horse loped along, her hair would wave up and down with the horse's gait. When they came over the hill in sight of the camp, my grandmother Davis saw the hair bouncing up and down and thought it was my mother's head bouncing, so she instantly surmised that her neck was broken and started to have hysterics. Fortunately, others promptly convinced her that such was not the case, and my mother was soon back in her mother's arms safe and sound.

They made the trip safely, and settled in an area called the "Delhi Flats." At the time, Mangum was the nearest town. It was about twenty or twenty-five miles from the Davis ranch-house home to Mangum. My mother grew up there and had little formal education. She was around cowboys much of her life and learned many of the old cowboy ballads which I remember her singing as she did the household chores when I was a small boy. This was the beginning of my appreciation of western ballads and later of country and western music. It was probably the beginning of my enjoyment of similar types of poetry. My mother died on January 23, 1973. After my parents were married, they lived for several years in Erick, Oklahoma, where my oldest sister, Agnes, and my older brother, Aubrey, were born. They moved to Vega, Texas, in 1914 when my father accepted a position as manager of the local lumber yard. He agreed to stay for at least one year. He and mother wound up spending the rest of their lives there. Two more girls and two more boys were born to them in Vega, making a total of six children in the family. The full names of the six children in my parents' family are listed in order of birth:

Agnes Elizabeth was born in Erick, Oklahoma on March 25, 1910. We called her by her first name, Agnes. She died in Amarillo, Texas on July 31, 1993.

James Aubrey was born January 14, 1912, in Erick, Oklahoma. We called him Aubrey. All of his adult life he was called "Hot Dog" by the residents of Vega. He died there on September 23, 1991.

Winelle Lorene was born November 27, 1914, in Vega. She died in Amarillo on October 16, 1986. She was called Winelle.

Bishop Davis was born December 28, 1919, in Vega. He is called Bishop or Bish.

William Dudley was born December 3, 1922, in Vega. We started calling him by his initials, W. D., but this soon was changed to "Dub."

Evelyn Rae was born June 18, 1926, in Vega. She is called Evelyn.

The earliest recollections I have of Vega are of a small, unincorporated town even though it was, and is, the county seat of Oldham County. Livestock roamed free on the town site. There was no gas, electricity or municipal water system. Each house had an outhouse behind it, and many houses had individual windmills.

We always kept a milk cow to provide milk and butter for the family, as did many others in the town, because there was no refrigeration, and the only milk deliveries were from a couple of farmers who lived near town and milked enough cows to provide daily milk deliveries to selected customers in town. After I was older and had a horse of my own, I made my spending money by gathering milk cows from various places in town each morning, driving them to a pasture near town, and then getting them from the pasture after school and driving them home. I charged one dollar per month per cow for this service. I usually had fifteen to twenty cows to pick up and deliver each day so I had a reasonable amount of spending money for those times. It was during the depression years when men were glad to get a job that paid a dollar and a half to two dollars a day.

The earliest thing I can remember happened when I was between one and two years of age. My parents said I was just a little over a year old at the time. My older brother, Aubrey, had a mare named Nellie, which he rode practically every day, and she was quite gentle. However, unbeknownst to my father, he had been letting other kids ride behind the saddle and deliberately put their feet in her flanks to make her buck. As a result, she got so she would start bucking when anyone got on behind the saddle.

One day Aubrey rode up with another boy, Wirt Burns, riding with him in the saddle. My father had me in his arms and told Aubrey to give me a ride on his horse. He handed me up to Aubrey, which made it pretty crowded in the saddle, so Aubrey told Wirt to get off, but my father told him just to move behind the saddle. As soon as Wirt moved behind the saddle, Old Nellie began to buck. She bucked across a barrow ditch in front of our house, and Wirt was thrown off into the muddy ditch. The horse quit bucking as soon as Wirt was thrown off.

There are two things I always remembered that were impressed in my mind. I remember seeing my father running up to the horse as she was bucking and trying to grab me off, and I remember seeing Wirt land on his hands and knees in the muddy ditch. I also remember Aubrey laughed when Wirt landed in the mud. In later years, I delighted in telling people I rode my first bucking horse when I was a little over one year old. Of course, no one believed me.

One morning after I had eaten breakfast and was ready to go out and play, Mother said, "You can't go out now. There is an old male out by the house." (Mother always said "male" instead of "bull." In those days, women of her generation were taught that a lady did not say "bull." They were to say "male" or "surly.") I looked out the living room window, and a very large, white bull was standing there looking as if he were looking through the window at me. He was standing not more than five yards from the house. I don't remember how long it was before he wandered off far enough that mother considered it was safe for me to go out.

As I said before, the town was not incorporated at that time, and there were no herd laws, so livestock roamed freely around the town. There were few fences, and there were still many wagons and horse-drawn buggies. There was a small herd of burros that ran free who nobody seemed to claim, so occasionally a boy would catch one, usually with the aid of several other boys, and claim it for his own until he got tired of it and turned it loose again. My brother, Aubrey, caught one, and broke it to harness to pull a sled which he had built.

One winter morning when there were about five inches of snow on the ground, Aubrey decided to take my younger brother, W. D., whom we called "Dub," and me for a ride on his donkey sled. Mother bundled us in warm clothing and Aubrey hitched the burro to the sled. It was a crude harness that he had rigged up himself. Dub was less than a year old at the time, so I would have been some less than four years old, and Aubrey would have been approximately 12 years old.

We went out to the sled, and Aubrey put me near the back with Dub in front of me. When Aubrey got seated on the sled in front of us and told the burro to "get up," it started backing up instead of going forward, which is not unusual for a burro. Aubrey stood up, stepped off the sled, and started slapping the burro on the rump with the reins to convince it to go forward. It kept backing up until it had both hind feet on the sled, and at that time I decided it was time to abandon ship. However, I was true to the old tradition of women and children first, because I decided I had to save the baby first. I remember Dub had on a red sweater and red toboggan cap. I reached over and got a handful of clothing right between his shoulder blades and flung him off the sled. The adrenaline must have been flowing because I turned him a complete flip in the air, and he landed sitting up in the snow just as he was sitting on the sled. I immediately followed him off the sled and Aubrey laughed as he was getting the burro under control and convinced to go forward. We remounted the sled and had a pretty nice, but short, sled ride.

About a year later, Aubrey had traded for a larger burro. He kept it in the cow lot behind our barn. One day a friend of his came to visit him. They went out in the alley behind our barn, and, of course, I always wanted to tag along with big brother, which caused some friction between us at times. However, this morning I was allowed to go with them. The three of us sat down behind the barn, and the burro was standing with his head over the fence into the alley. Aubrey and his friend started telling ghost stories, and I was really taking them in. My brother's friend was telling a really scary ghost story, and just as he got to the climax when I imagined something terrible was about to happen, the jackass decided to bray. For those who may not have heard a jackass bray at close range, I will say it is a pretty awesome sound. Coming when it did, it scared hell out of me. I think I grabbed Aubrey around the neck and I actually felt the hair standing up on the back of my neck. At least, it felt like it was. Aubrey and his friend were quite startled at first also. Then we all had a big laugh.

When I was very small, we had a shepherd dog which, of course, we called "Old Shep." It is the first dog I remember. It was very good with children, and I remember riding it at times like a horse for a short distance. I remember one time when I was on his back and my father was beside me. Another person came up and Old Shep got excited and started jumping around and threw me off. It hurt me enough that I cried.

In the summer time, the children went barefoot. I remember how tender my feet were when I first took my shoes off in the spring. However, it did not take long for them to get toughened so we could walk around barefoot with no problems until we came to a sticker patch. We had a type of stickers we called "bullhead" or "goathead" stickers. They grow on a vine on the ground. The stickers grow on a thick pancake-like sort of seed pod which, upon maturity, broke up into tetrahedron-shaped seeds with two thorns, or stickers, on each seed. The two stickers resembled two rather sturdy horns protruding from two points of the tetrahedron. From their shape comes the name. To me, they look more like a bull's head than a goat's head, but "goathead" has come to be the name used most. When we came to a patch of these stickers that were still green, they would stick in my feet, but Old Shep's foot pads were thick enough that they did not bother him, so I would call Old Shep and ride him across the sticker patch.

Although my father was manager of a lumber yard, which was considered to be a pretty good job, we lived at what would be considered "poverty level" these days. My father did not like to go very much in debt. He saved enough money in the first four years he was in Vega to buy a vacated newspaper building which was converted to our home. It had a flat roof and no partitions inside except for a small room that had been partitioned off as an office. I was the first one of the family born in that house.

My first remembrance was of some "rooms" partitioned off with large, green burlap curtains. The flat roof was replaced with a gable roof before I was born, I think, but the house was finally actually partitioned to make a six room house when I was between four and five years old. It was remodeled in front to have a screened-in porch. Three of the rooms had plaster walls, and three had wooden walls covered with wallpaper. The kitchen walls were covered with oilcloth, so they could be easily washed. There were three bedrooms, a living room, dining room, and a kitchen. It was a "shotgun" type house—that being a long, comparatively narrow house with the front door at one end, the back door at the other end, and no side doors. We had coal stoves for both heating and cooking at first, but later, we had a kerosene cook stove. We usually just had one bath per week, especially during winter. Water was heated on the cook stove, and we bathed in a No. 3 wash tub which was also used when mother washed clothes using a rub board to get them clean. I remember some of our clothes were boiled in a vessel designed for that purpose which fit over two burners on the kerosene stove. I think it was our underwear, the bed sheets, and pillow cases which were boiled when they were washed in order to sterilize them. My mother worked very hard in those days.

When I was four and a half years old, my mother and father along with my younger brother, W. D. (Dub) and myself took a trip with Mr. Hale, who ran a grocery store in Vega, to the site of a famous Indian battle in Hutchinson County, Texas, about twenty miles northeast of present-day Borger, Texas, and approximately ninety-five miles from Vega. The trip was for the purpose of commemorating the 50th anniversary of the battle which occurred on June 27, 1874, at a place called Adobe Walls.

I remember we left early in the morning of June 26. It was still dark when we started out. I don't know what kind of car Mr. Hale was driving, but it was a sedan. The things I remember on the way from Vega to the battle site are few. I remember going through Amarillo and noticing the streets were paved with brick—the first paved streets I had seen. From Amarillo to the old battle site was on what we call "rut" roads. They were roads made by wagons and automobiles passing in the same place and made bare ruts in the grass. There were no route markings so sometimes when there was a fork in the road, there was some discussion between my father and Mr. Hale as to which trail to take. It was by guess, because I don't think either one of them had traveled the road before.

In late afternoon, we reached the Canadian River, and we had to ford it to get to the battle site. The Canadian River has a wide, sandy bed approximately one quarter of a mile wide. When there has been no rain for a week or two, the water is less than two feet deep and maybe twenty yards wide. However, the sand is very soft, so it is easy to get a car stuck in the sand. I remember that we got stuck, but there were men stationed there in the river bed to push cars that got stuck. With the help of four or five men pushing, we made it across the river and selected a place to camp for the night. By that time, there were a lot of people there.

I remember a few things about the festivities the next day, June 27, 1924. I remember being with my parents when they met my mother's oldest sister, Sally, who was also there with part of her family for the festivities. (She had nine children, with thirty years difference between the ages of the oldest and the youngest.) As I remember, there was a wall of one of the old buildings still standing, and it was in front of that where people made speeches. The widow of Billy Dixon spoke. He was a famous Indian fighter and buffalo hunter, who fought in this battle and later, as an Army scout, won the Congressional Medal of Honor in another Indian fight. Of course, I don't remember anything about the speeches. A granite marker engraved with the names of the settlers who fought in the battle was dedicated.

I don't remember anything else about the trip until we got back to Amarillo. I was asleep in the back seat of the car when I was suddenly thrown onto the floor when we had a collision with a Model T Ford. Fortunately, not much damage was done. Cars didn't go very fast in those days. I remember Mr. Hale and the other man arguing for a while about whose fault it was. Anyway, we soon proceeded on our way and made it back home. The distance from Vega to the old Adobe Walls site is approximately ninety-five miles, and it took almost an entire day to drive it due to the condition of the roads, as well as the slow speed of the cars in those days.

In August of 1977, I took my wife and three children to the site. We drove from Pampa, Texas, to the site and back one afternoon. The only indications of the site now are several stone markers. It struck me that the time between my first visit there and my second visit with my family was approximately fifty-three years, which was three more than the elapsed time between the date of the battle and my first visit. It would be about the same time lapse as visiting a World War II battle site today.

When I was about six years old, I became a friend to another boy approximately my age whose parents ran the wagon yard and also the dray wagon for the town. This boy's name is Arthur Campsey, who was called "Son" by everyone, including his family. Their house was near the wagon yard. I would go to this house pretty regularly. He was a member of quite a large family, and his mother bought peanut butter in about a five-pound pail. Son and I would quite often get the bucket of peanut butter and some crackers and retreat into their garage and eat large amounts of peanut butter and crackers. The garage was a separate building, and I don't remember that they actually used it for a garage. I don't remember whether or not they even had a car at that time. There was a pile of old papers and magazines in the garage. One day when Son and I had retreated to the garage, Son brought some matches he had snitched from the kitchen. We decided to build a small fire with the papers. Well, as often happens when kids play with matches, the fire got out of control. I think a puff of wind blew a piece of the burning paper in our fire over to the larger pile of papers. When the smoke and fire in the garage indicated to me that things had gone beyond our control, I headed for home at a full gallop. The members of the Campsey family who were at home managed to put out the fire before it burned anything except the papers, but I stayed away from there for several days before I gingerly ventured back, with Son's assurance that nothing would happen to me. Mrs. Campsey lived to a ripe old age, and up to the last time I saw her in 1946, she still kidded me about setting her garage on fire and eating up her peanut butter.

A short time later, the Campseys moved to a farm south of Vega, and the wagon yard was closed. It was torn down soon after that, and a farm implement company was built in its place. The automobile was rapidly displacing teams and wagons. I remember, however, that gypsy caravans came through Vega in covered wagons for several years after that before they converted to automobiles. They camped by the railroad stock pens in the east side of town.

At about the same time in the late 1920s, farmers began to change from live horsepower to mechanical horsepower by means of farm tractors. The first farm tractors I remember were the old steam powered Rumley tractors. I don't remember exactly what fuel they used to fire the boiler, but it would have to have been coal or oil because there was no firewood available on the treeless plains. Coal was shipped in by rail from around Walsenburg, Colorado, in those days. There was an oil refinery built in Amarillo after oil was discovered around Borger and Pampa, Texas, in 1926. It was in the late 1920s and early 1930s that the grassland was plowed up and made into large wheat farms. After International Harvester Company introduced gasoline powered tractors and John Deere Company introduced its tractors powered by kerosene, cultivated farms became larger. Very few farms were smaller than one section (640 acres or one square mile).

Although most of the flat plains prairie land was put to the plow, all of the land in a wide strip across the Texas Panhandle which we call the Canadian River Breaks remained ranch land. This was a strip of rolling hills and eroded land on each side of the Canadian River which was not suited to large scale farming. The Landergin Brothers ranch was the largest ranch that shipped cattle from Vega in those days. I remember seeing herds of cattle that would stretch for two miles or more being driven down the roads into Vega from the north. There were about 2000 head in such a herd. They were taken to the stock pens in the east part of town and shipped out by the train load. Once they started loading a train, work continued until it was full. I remember hearing the cowboys yelling until late into the night sometimes when they were completing the loading of a train so it could pull out. The ranchers wanted the cattle to be on the train as short a time as possible since there was no feed or water available from the time they were loaded until they were unloaded. Most of the cattle shipped from Vega in those days went to Kansas City, Kansas.

At this time, I developed a burning desire to be a cowboy. Cowboys were my heroes as I was growing up. There were still hitching posts by some of the downtown stores, and there were wooden sidewalks.

After the Campseys moved to their farm, I continued to be close friends with Son. I loved to spend time on the farm with him and ride horses. I didn't have a horse until several years later. The Campseys had several horses, so sometimes Son would ride one to town and lead one for me to ride. We always rode bareback because neither of us had our own saddle at that time.

Son and I remained close friends all the way through high school until we went separate ways in the Army during World War II. We are still close friends, but we only see each other once each year when we both attend the Oldham County Roundup in Vega.

I started to school in September of 1927. I was almost eight years old when I started because in those days there were only eleven grades in public school in Texas. Seven years, grades one through seven, were elementary, or grammar, school, and four years were high school. All grades were in one school building. The first year I attended, each room was heated by a coal stove. There were two large outdoor toilets, one for girls, and one for boys. I can't remember what the drinking fountains were like. There was a football field, and an outdoor basketball court. I remember seeing the high school girls (including my sister, Agnes) playing basketball on the outdoor court. It was not surfaced in any way. Like the football field, it was bare ground. The girls wore white blouses and large billowy, black bloomers.

I was quite intimidated by the older boys when I started to school and hesitated to enter games at recess in a group where older boys were playing. I soon got over being intimidated, but I was always rather quiet and shy. However, I was not as much so as one boy I remember. His mother had to come and sit in the classroom all day. If she went out to go to the restroom, he would cry until she came back. I don't remember how long she had to do that before he was finally convinced he would be safe without her. My first year in school, the first and second grades were in the same room.

During the summer after my first year in school, a new school building was constructed. The old school building was expanded, remodeled, and converted entirely to classrooms. A basement was added for a coal-fired furnace, and a steam heating system was installed. A new and larger elevated water tank was installed. The school had its own windmill to supply water. A complete new plumbing system with indoor restrooms and drinking fountains was installed. A wing was added with a gymnasium below and an auditorium above. The floor of the gymnasium was approximately ten feet below ground level. The dressing rooms were below ground level, with shower rooms above the dressing rooms at ground level. We thought the new school building was wonderful.

About the time the Campseys moved to the country, a family moved into the house across the alley from us. They had two children, a boy and a girl. The girl was about three years older than the boy. The boy, Jim Bales, was approximately two years younger than I and a year older than my brother, Dub. The three of us played together all the time and became very good friends. There will be a lot more about him later.

I think it was some time in the spring of 1927 that Frederick H. Krahn came to Vega from Illinois to work for his brother, Everett, who had married a local girl and was farming his mother-in-law's land. Fred met and started dating my sister, Agnes. They began going steady and one morning about ten o'clock, he and Agnes drove up in a car. Agnes came inside and went to her room. Mother followed her, and I could hear them talking. It must have been a Saturday morning because I wasn't in school, and my father was at work in the lumber yard. Aubrey was not at home at the time. In a short time, Agnes came out with a suitcase and mother was following her, crying. Agnes went out, got in the car with Fred, and they left. Mother continued to cry, so all of the kids started crying too. I suppose Winelle knew what was going on, but none of the rest of us had the foggiest idea. We were only crying because mother was.

Right at this time, Jim Bales came in our back door and on into the living room. He came to Dub first and asked him why he was crying. Dub said, "I don't know." Jim then approached me with a worried look and asked me the same question and got the same answer. He looked at us all worriedly and decided it was time for him to retreat out the back door. He went home and told his mother something terrible was going on at our house. She checked and found out it wasn't all that bad. Mother regained her composure and explained to us as best she could that Agnes was going away to get married and wouldn't live with us anymore. They got married January 28, 1928. We all settled down then in our normal behavior. When my father came home for dinner (as we called the noon meal, which everyone now calls "lunch"), mother said to him, "Your oldest daughter just ran off to get married." Dad thought a moment and said, "Well, I would have liked it better if she had finished high school first." That was all he said. After a week or so, Fred and Agnes came back from their honeymoon. They settled down in Vega and lived there for many years. All five of their children, all boys, were born in Vega. Their fourth child was stillborn, but the other four were very healthy and are still living. All were born at home with our old family doctor in attendance.

It was not nearly so traumatic when the rest of us got married.

The Bales family had moved from the house near us to an apartment in the Oldham Hotel, which was on the courthouse square in Vega and only two blocks from our house. A family by the name of Hindman moved into the house where the Bales family had lived. They had a boy named Marvin who was their only child. We became very close friends. His father, Joe Hindman, ran a wholesale petroleum products station for a time. It was the first Continental

Oil Company wholesale station in Vega, and he was its first manager. There were a good number of cars on the highway by that time. There were three "filling stations" in town then. Filling stations primarily just filled cars and trucks with gasoline and oil, but provided no other service. Later on, they began furnishing free air for tires, started fixing flats, changing oil, etc. Then they began to be called "service stations."

Joe Hindman sold the wholesale petroleum products station and went into the cattle business. He first leased a small ranch approximately 25 miles west of Vega. It had a small two room house on it where they lived part of the time when there was a lot of work to be done with the cattle. Sometimes they would ask me to stay a week with them because Marvin would get lonely with no other child around. I was really in "hog heaven," as they used to say, when I was staying with him. We got to ride horses every day and sometimes help with rounding up the cattle in one pasture and moving them to another.

The house where the Hindmans lived in Vega had a barn and corral which was just across the alley from our barn. Marvin had a beautiful paint horse, named "Old Paint," of course, which he kept in town most of the time, and he would let my younger brother, Dub, and me ride at times.

At one time, Mr. Hindman bought a small herd of Shetland ponies. There was a stallion and perhaps thirty mares. They were unbroken, so he hired a couple of cowboys to break them so he could sell them for kid ponies. He brought two of them which had been ridden until they wouldn't buck any more, but were not yet gentle, and put them in his corral in Vega. Marvin and I, along with others who volunteered, were supposed to ride them and gentle them. I remember one day I was riding the one called "Tiny" in the corral when she suddenly reared and fell backwards on top of me. Fortunately, she was appropriately named, and weighed only about 250 pounds, so I was not hurt. I was lucky in that the saddle horn hit on my belt buckle and sort of slipped off on one side of my stomach and did not dig in. That combined with the pony's light weight kept me from being hurt. I don't think the Shetland pony business proved to be profitable because Mr. Hindman sold all of them after a year or two.

I don't remember anything unusual during my first four years of school. I made good grades and became less timid. In fact, I was a little monster at times, I guess, and I got my share of spankings. I did not say anything at home when I got a spanking at school, because when I started to school, my father told me that if he heard of my getting a spanking there, he would give me another one when I got home. I will say that my father spanked me only one time in my life and that was because I disobeyed him and then ran from him when he started toward me.

I remember three things which happened that impressed me when I was in the fifth grade in school.

Early one morning I was awakened by a ambulance siren. I had never heard one before. We were all curious as to what had happened. The ambulance sped on through Vega. The highway, Route 66, was a graded dirt road through Vega, and at that time it ran through town. There were two ninety-degree turns in town, one at the bank on the northwest corner of the courthouse square, and the other at the school house on the opposite side of the railroad tracks. For this reason, the driver of the ambulance kept his siren on all through Vega.

When I went to school, the ambulance was the main topic of conversation. I found out it was carrying "Boss" Jackson, who had been shot in a gambling house in Santa Rosa, New Mexico, which is about one hundred miles west of Vega. The ambulance took him to a hospital in Amarillo, Texas, which is thirty-five miles east of Vega. This made his total ambulance ride about 135 miles, and most of it was on unpaved road. Everyone wondered why he did not go to the hospital in Tucumcari, New Mexico, since the ambulance passed right through there. In fact, the ambulance was probably based in Tucumcari.

"Boss" Jackson had lived in Vega for many, many, years, and was one of the town's shady characters. He always wanted to be the town "tough," after he had served time in the penitentiary for killing a man, but he was known to have backed down several times when someone he was trying to bully challenged him. He and another man from Vega had gone to Santa Rosa, and were running a gambling house there. A man came in during the early morning hours and shot Boss five times in the chest. After riding all that distance in the ambulance, he survived and was apparently going to recover, when he developed pneumonia, as often happens in hospitals. They had no antibiotics nor any other effective treatment for pneumonia in those days, so he died and was buried in the Vega cemetery.

Another exciting thing that happened in 1932 was the armed robbery of the first State Bank in Vega. It was the only bank, of course.

One day at noon, I was walking home from school to eat lunch. Our house was about four blocks north of the school, and one block north of the bank. I walked past the bank on the way to and from school. On the day of the robbery, I walked past the bank, and at the next street intersection, a brand new shiny car was parked. A man was standing on its right side with one foot on the running board, and looking down the street toward the bank. He was wearing a big, white cowboy hat and cowboy boots. As I passed behind the car, he really looked me over. Finally, he said, "Howdy," out of the left corner of his mouth. I said, "Howdy," and walked on to our house, which was about one-half block from where the car was parked. I didn't think any more about it, but in a few minutes, my father came in, having come from the lumber yard for lunch. He said to my mother, "I wonder what those men in that car are up to."

As my father walked past them, the man got in the car. They drove around the block and came by the front of the bank, on up the street past our house, turned right at the next block, drove about a block east, and stopped again, where they could see the front of the bank.

All of the family who were home for lunch then sat down and ate. I finished my lunch and walked back to school, passing the bank again, and noticing nothing out of the ordinary.

After we returned to our classrooms after lunch, I noticed three teachers out in the hall acting very excited. Our teacher came into the classroom and told us the bank had been robbed and that the robbers had taken the bank clerk, Bob Armitage, with them as a hostage.

The robbers had apparently "cased the joint" very thoroughly before the robbery. Since no one had remembered seeing the actual robbers before, it was believed they had local help. They knew what time the time vault at the bank would be open; they also apparently knew that each Wednesday at noon, the cashier and assistant cashier both went to lunch at the Kiwanis Club meeting on the second floor of the two-story building across the street from the bank, and that the bank clerk would be alone in the bank during that time.

As best I can determine based on timing, I believe I walked past the bank just after the robbery and before it was reported. If so, there were four men locked in the vault of the bank at the time I walked by it on my way back to school. When I walked back, the robbers' car was nowhere to be seen, and there was no activity at the bank when I passed it.

The third thing I remember vividly from 1932 is the beginning of the "black dusters" of the dust bowl days. I think the period from 1932 to 1937 are called the "Dust Bowl" years.

After the stock market crash in 1929, the Great Depression began. Prices began falling. The rains were good in the Texas Panhandle in 1930, 1931, and 1932. The farmers raised good wheat crops, but prices had fallen so low, they made little or no money. They tried to beat the price by planting more wheat until, in 1931, I remember wheat piled in large piles on the ground because the storage facilities were insufficient, and there were not enough freight cars available to move the wheat as fast as it was being hauled in. The price fell to eighteen cents per bushel. Farmers tried feeding the grain to hogs, cattle, and chickens, but then livestock prices hit bottom.

Then on top of these hard times a drought set in that developed into the worst on record. The prevailing winds in the Texas Panhandle are from the southwest, and in the spring of 1932, when the March winds began to blow, it seemed that every day there would be more dust in the air.

One day while we were in school, the wind seemed to get higher and higher, and the dust got thicker. It got heavy enough to require lights to be turned on in the school building.

The school superintendent became worried, and had all the classroom teachers bring the children into the gymnasium. I assume he thought we would be safer there in case of a tornado since the gymnasium was partially below ground level. We liked that idea and were having a wonderful time playing in the gym, even though the air was a little dusty. I remember looking up in the seats in the gymnasium, and one of the teachers was crying. Two other teachers were trying to console her. She had became very scared apparently at what the weather was doing.

Shortly before time for school to let out, the wind slackened some, and we went back to our classrooms. When I walked home from school that day, the wind was still blowing pretty hard, and there was a lot of static electricity. I noticed the leaves on some bushes had turned black. At one telephone pole I passed, sparks were jumping on one of the insulators and making a cracking sound.

Well, this was just one sandstorm of many more to come, and they got increasingly worse. The drought continued, and each spring when the spring winds came, the soil blew more each year. The "blow dirt," as we called it, drifted like snow to form drifts, or dunes, that covered fences and farm machinery, and almost covered some farm outbuildings. The tumbleweeds would blow against the barbed wire fences, farm machinery, outbuildings, etc., and then they would start catching some of the blowing soil and start a drift which eventually covered them.

I believe 1935 was the worst year for the "black dusters." These would come rolling in with a huge dust cloud that resembled the recent pictures of volcanic dust coming down the sides of Mt. Pinatubo in the Philippines. Of course, they were not that bad, but they looked very ominous. When they hit, everything went black, and one could not see his hand in front of his face. Anyone caught outside away from home would became disoriented and would have to stop and wait for it to blow over.

I remember one of the worst ones blew in from the west one Sunday afternoon in early March, 1935. It was the first one, I think, where there was total darkness, which lasted only a few minutes, although the blowing dust lasted much longer.

Another of the very worst black dusters blew in on April 14, 1935. Ironically, it was also on a Sunday, but it was about six thirty in the evening, I think. I have seen many pictures published which were taken of this black, rolling cloud as it approached, and it looked awesome. We saw it coming and our family started wetting towels and placing them around the windows to keep out dust. When it hit, there was immediate complete darkness. In spite of our efforts, quite a lot of dust got into the house. With the lights on, it was hazy, like a fog, in the house. I don't know how long the blackout lasted that time. It was still dark at the time normal darkness would occur after the sun went down and was still blowing hard when I went to bed.

It was during this period of the dust bowl years that the mass exodus of the tenant farmers occurred in Kansas, Oklahoma, the Texas Panhandle, and parts of New Mexico and Colorado. This was the basis of John Steinbeck's novel, *The Grapes of Wrath*, about the exodus of "Okies" from Oklahoma to California.

I could probably write a full-length novel about the things I remember from the dust bowl and depression years, but I will only describe a few things that impressed me.

Concerning the blowing dust, it occurred every spring for several years. Sometimes it would start in February and continue on into May. I remember each morning when I walked to school the sky would be clear and the sun would be shining. It would be such a wonderful morning and I would just pray that it would stay like that all day. It very seldom did. Usually by about ten o'clock in the morning the wind would get up and start blowing from the southwest. By noon, the dust would be blowing enough to make it very uncomfortable to be outside. We would go home for dinner (lunch) and mother would have it set on the dining table with a table cloth spread over it to keep the dust out of the food and our plates. We would keep the food in the serving dishes covered and only uncover a dish long enough to spoon out servings on our plates.

In spite of our efforts, we still ate a lot of dust when we were both inside and outside because of the dust in the air. It would cake in my nose, and I could feel the grit on my teeth much of the time.

I remember hearing a song on the radio a few times which was a parody of the song "Beautiful Texas." I have always remembered a part of the chorus, as follows:

Oh beautiful, beautiful Texas
Where the wind and the dirt do blow,
We ought to like this country
We have it to eat, you know.

The editor of the Amarillo, Texas newspaper wrote a humorous column titled *The Tactless Texan*, and in it, he called himself "Old Tack." He began touting the Panhandle air as being good for one because it was rich in Vitamin K. It helped people cope by making light of it as much as possible. There were numerous dust storm jokes.

The cattle would have a streak of mud from their eyes all the way down to the bottoms of their lower jaws. The blowing dust made their eyes water, and the tears caught the dust to make the mud.

In the drought, livestock began to starve. The government set up a program to buy the cattle. Those that were strong enough to be driven to the stock yards were shipped east to canneries. They were slaughtered and canned. The canned meat was then shipped out over the country to be given to the unemployed as relief. Cattle and hogs too poor to ship were bought by the government, killed on the range, and left for the buzzards. I don't remember for sure what the government paid for them, but it seems that I remember a price of three dollars per head for weaned calves and up to fifteen dollars per head for cattle that could be shipped. I saw many trainloads passing through Vega from the west and others being shipped from Vega.

There were many government "make work" programs. The most prominent were the Works Progress Administration (WPA) and the Civilian Conservation Corps (CCC). The CCC was for young men who would normally be of military age. My brother, Aubrey, served a year in a CCC camp near Cuchillo, New Mexico, and helped complete a lot of useful projects that were of lasting benefit.

The drought continued until 1937 and, although it was very aggravating to be outside during one of the dust storms, they were not the blinding "black dusters" of 1935.

During the depression years, there were many men coming through Vega riding freight trains or hitch-hiking on Route 66. Most of them were headed west to California looking for work, but some of them had been there, did not find work, and were heading back east. Many stopped in Vega for a short time to beg for food. It seemed like almost every day someone would knock at our door and ask for something to eat. Mother always gave them something if she had any leftovers or prepared food. There were transient camps established by the federal government where transients out of work could live for a limited period of time.

We were lucky in that my father had a job all during the depression, but his salary was cut to sixty dollars per month, so we had to skimp and be very frugal, because there were five children in the family who were living at home much of the time. Although my parents objected, Aubrey dropped out of high school and did not graduate. He found work at times as a cowboy or farmhand, but was unemployed much of the time. As I mentioned before, he spent one year in a CCC camp.

We could get by because everything was very cheap when compared to the present time. For example, canned salmon was ten cents per can, bacon was about ten cents per pound, dried pinto beans were about five cents per pound, bread was five cents a loaf, and milk was ten cents a quart. As a result, we never went hungry, but we ate a lot of pinto beans, and we had very few new clothes.

My brother, Dub, and I worked together in the job I mentioned earlier of gathering milk cows in the morning, taking them to pasture before school and then going after school to take them from the pasture and deliver them back to their barns in town. This was after I got my own horse in 1934.

My father had promised me a few years earlier when times were not so bad that he would buy me a horse if I was valedictorian of my class when I graduated from grammar school. He kept his promise although I am sure it strained the budget. He bought me a very pretty bay half-thoroughbred mare. I called her Ribbon, and she was my pride and joy for years.

We had several dogs during the time I was growing up in Vega, but the two most memorable were Old Shep, whom I have mentioned before, and Old Bullet. We had both of them longer than any of the others.

Old Bullet was a bulldog. I don't know what breed he was, but he was not a purebred, I am sure. He resembled what I would imagine as a cross between a bull terrier and a boxer. He was very muscular, and would fight any dog he considered to be encroaching on his territory around our home or getting too close to members of our family. He never even acted like he would bite a human, and was a very friendly dog. I don't remember exactly when my brother, Aubrey, got him, but it was in the late 1920s. Aubrey had an old Model T Ford, and he would take Bullet hunting with him when he went rabbit or duck hunting. Old Bullet would get on a front fender between the fender and the hood and brace himself so he would not fall off when the car turned.

Several years later, Old Bullet was poisoned, and we had to watch him die in our back yard. Both he and Old Shep were poisoned, but Old Shep died at night. I was only a small boy when Old Shep died, but I was in high school when Old Bullet died.

As a result of having the two dogs I loved most die from poisoning, I have a deep hatred and loathing for anyone who would poison a dog. We had no idea who did it or why.

Each year we go to Vega for the annual Oldham County Roundup which is on the second Saturday in August. People who live in Oldham County now and those who have lived there in the past, along with friends, relatives or strangers, gather on the courthouse lawn and visit. It is a big reunion of old friends. There is a free barbecue at noon. The barbecue plates served invariably consist of barbecued beef, pinto beans, sliced onion, pickles, stewed dried apricots, and two slices of white bread. Area ranchers donate the beef. Contributions are collected during the year to buy the other food, and the day before, volunteer townspeople prepare twenty to thirty gallons of pinto beans and fifteen to twenty gallons of dried apricots. They barbecue five beeves, and usually about 2,000 people are served. There is always plenty for everyone, and people can go back for more until it runs out or everyone is full. Before the lunch is served there is a parade with floats and many beautiful quarter horses.

In the early days of Vega, all of the business buildings were wooden frame construction, except for the Oldham Hotel on the northeast corner of the square and a two-story building on the northwest corner of the square. The sidewalks were made of wood. There were two large fires which occurred in the business area on the courthouse square.

The first large fire on the square occurred on May 8, 1932. The fire started in a recently constructed two-story hotel about the middle of the block on the west side of the square. The wind was from the north at the time, and the men fighting the fire with very little water managed to save the buildings to the north of the hotel where the fire started, but all the businesses to the south of that building were destroyed. There were six buildings destroyed. There was concern for a while that the lumber yard my father managed would burn. It was approximately one-half block west of the nearest building to it which burned down. It got so hot that one of the plate glass windows in the front of the store cracked.

I was in school at the time. The school was located two blocks south of the block where the fire was burning. School was disrupted and all of us went to the north classrooms and watched the fires. It was all over by the time school let out, but it was still hot enough that I had to change my route home from school. I usually walked up the street on the block where the fire was.

Another fire occurred on the north side of the square on July 5, 1931. Two buildings burned, but the bucket brigade miraculously managed to save the other frame buildings.

After these fires, all wooden sidewalks were replaced by concrete sidewalks. All buildings built on the square after that were of brick construction. Some of the lots where buildings were before the fire are still vacant. It is ironic that a bond issue was voted in February, 1931, for a municipal water system for Vega, but it had not been constructed at the time of the fires.

The city purchased the site and equipment where the small water system operated by Col. J. T. Owens was located. It was just across the street and less than one-half block south from our home. I watched with fascination as the huge water tower and tank were constructed. At the same time, a ditching machine was digging deep ditches and about eight-inch cast iron water mains were installed.

When the system was completed, I was amazed at the water pressure we had. The city purchased a new Model T Ford fire truck. It was kept in a large barn belonging to a farm machinery dealer. The machinery barn had been constructed on part of the old wagon yard. Of course, the truck had to be cranked by hand to start it, and the battery was not kept charged, so it got to the point that when there was a fire, someone with a pickup truck usually tied on to the fire truck and pulled it to the fire. This rig seldom got to a fire in time to put it out, but it was useful in containing the fire to one building.

After World War II, the city of Vega purchased a surplus fire truck from Amarillo Air Force Base, which was scheduled to be closed. That truck was kept in running shape all the time. I don't know who bought the old Model T Ford truck, but it was practically in mint condition because it had been kept inside all the time, and the engine had been run very little. They used to get it in running shape every Christmas, and fire it up for Santa Claus to ride on to the community Christmas tree where he passed out stockings full of nuts, candy, and fruit to all of the children to be sure every child in town got something for Christmas.

After the water tower was constructed, it was painted a dull red color. It is much more attractive today. When I was about fifteen years old, some of the boys I ran around with started climbing the water tower at night. They ventured higher and higher until they got up the walk-around platform at the bottom of the tank itself. One night, I decided I had to be as brave as the others, so I climbed up to the platform. It was about three feet wide and had a guard rail about waist high so no one would be likely to fall off. I got off the ladder onto the walkway and looked down on the south side. It seemed as if I was looking straight down at the street on the north side of the courthouse square. I got scared and backed up with my back against the tank. I walked sideways around the tank with my back against the tank, got back on the ladder and carefully climbed back down to the ground. I never climbed it again but I was proud to boast that I had climbed up to the walkway and walked all the way around the tank on it. Some of the guys climbed all the way on top of the tank to the round ball on top, but I never attempted that.

My high school years in Vega were rather uneventful. There was not much for high school students to do in those days. The Depression was on, and none of us had much money to spend. We made our own entertainment most of the time. When we could get enough money together, we would take trips to Amarillo for more exciting things to do. My family had no car when I was in high school, so I had to depend upon others for transportation. Among my friends, there was usually one who could use the family car when three or four of us could get together to go to Amarillo on a Saturday night.

I was not very athletic. I was always tall and thin for my age. Football was the only sport I was really interested in playing. My brother, Aubrey, was of more stocky build than I was and so was my younger brother, W. D. (Dub). Aubrey was good enough to make the football team his freshman year in high school, and he played four years before he dropped out of school during his senior year.

I went out for football during my freshman year and didn't even make the traveling squad. I played very little in my sophomore year, and barely lettered my junior year. I persisted and made the first string my senior year. I was able to play high school football only because I was in a small town, and the pool of talent was very limited.

However, I have always been proud of the fact that during my senior year, I was the only one on the team who played every down of every game. We played eleven games that year and won nine of them.

I was six feet, two inches tall and weighed 145 pounds. One would expect a player of that build to play end, but I wasn't fast enough or good enough at catching passes. I played center on offense and line backer on defense. The rules of the game were very different in those days from the present game. Very little substitution was allowed. No more than three substitutes could go in at one time, and any player who left the game could not go back in until the next quarter. The team quarterback had to call the plays, and coaching from the sideline was not allowed. A substitute player coming into the game had to report to the referee. If his team had the ball, the referee went to the huddle with him to be sure he did not speak until after the next down was played. Football was a very different, and I think a rougher, game then. I believe that the rigorous physical training I received and the fortitude I developed while training for and playing football, as well as the hard physical work I did while working as a cowboy and farm hand before I joined the army, were the major factors in the ability of my mind and body to withstand the abuses I was subjected to during World War II.

After I graduated from high school in May of 1938, I decided I did not have a chance to attend college because my parents were certainly unable to pay the expenses. In those days a much smaller percentage of high school graduates entered college than is the case now.

I worked as a farmhand harvesting wheat and plowing during the summer of 1938. In August, I was offered a job by the Western Lumber and Hardware Company, which was the company my father had worked for since 1914. I was offered the position as manager of their store in Erick, Oklahoma. I accepted the job with some trepidation. Although I had learned a lot about the business and knew their bookkeeping system from helping my father and hanging around the lumber yard in Vega, I had never been away from home, and the farthest I had been from Vega was when my senior class took a trip to the Carlsbad Caverns in New Mexico.

The president of the company, Mr. George Woodward, wanted me to come to the headquarters office in Oklahoma City for a briefing before I went to the job location in Erick.

I boarded the east-bound Rock Island train that August morning and headed for Oklahoma City, 300 miles away. I left Vega about seven in the morning and arrived in Oklahoma City at about two that afternoon, as I remember.

When I stepped off the train, Mrs. Woodward was there to meet me, for which I was very grateful. As she was guiding me through the train station, the likes of which I had never seen before, she told me that my father had apparently been worried about me because he had called the office twice that day to be sure someone would meet me at the station and warned them that I had never been far from Vega by myself.

We got in her car, and as she drove through the city, I saw street cars and heavier traffic than I had ever seen. She took me to their home and showed me to my room. It was a very nice house. I stayed with them that night, went with Mr. Woodward to his office the next day to be briefed, stayed with them the next night, and left for Erick the next morning by bus. I was very impressed with the Woodward home and standard of living. They had a maid to prepare and serve their meals. Mrs. Woodward had a little silver bell on the table which she would ring when she wanted maid service. Real uptown for a country kid. They were very nice to me.

Fortunately for me, my mother's oldest living sister at that time lived in Erick. I got off the bus there rather late at night, and all the places of business were closed. I did not know how to get to my aunt's home. There were three or four men sitting on a curb near where the bus dropped me off, so I approached them and asked if one of them knew where my aunt, Mrs. Martha Gardner, lived. One of the men knew and gave me directions how to get there. It was about eight or ten blocks away, so I started walking. I came to a house that I thought fit the description the man gave me. The house was dark, but I knocked on the door. A woman came to the door, and a strange voice said, "Who is it?." I apologized and told her who I was looking for. She told me my aunt's home was about a block further up the street. I found the correct house on the next try, and my aunt came to the door when I knocked. She was glad to see me, but not as glad as I was to see her, I think.

I made arrangements for room and board at my aunt's home at a very reasonable price.

I found that the lumber yard was within easy walking distance from my aunt's home. I went to the lumber yard the next day and met the manager who was resigning, and he filled me in on the situation.

Erick was a small town with a population of approximately two thousand people. There were three lumber yards there and not enough business for one, so all of them were losing money. The manager had found another job because he figured the lumber yard would be closed within a short period of time.

Within a day or two, a man from the company headquarters came to take inventory to check me in and the old manager out. The old manager wished me luck and left.

Well, I found out there was truly very little business. I was so young that when anyone came in and asked to see the manager, they could hardly believe it when I told them I was it. I was eighteen years old at the time, and looked even younger.

It rocked along for about eight months, and I could easily handle the small amount of business I had. One day in early March, the company auditor, Mr. F. B. Burke, walked into the store and told me he had come to help me close out the store. We advertised a quitting business sale, and business really picked up. We got a company truck from the yard in Elk City, Oklahoma, to make deliveries and haul some of the fixtures to another company yard in Texola, Oklahoma.

By the end of March, we had everything moved out and ready to vacate the building. I was back in Vega by early April.

When I returned to Vega, I found the grass was greening up, and we were having a lot of April showers. The range land in the Canadian River Breaks was looking good. Due to the long drought and depressed prices, the Landergin Brothers ranch had gone broke, and an insurance company had foreclosed on the land. Most of their thousands of head of cattle had been sold.

For a week or two, I had noticed a stranger driving around town in an expensive automobile. I found out his name was Jack Mansfield, and that he was a rancher from south Texas. It turned out that south Texas and northern Mexico were in a severe drought, and he was looking for grass.

He made a deal with the insurance company to lease that portion of the Landergin Brothers ranch known as their "North Ranch." It consisted of nearly three hundred thousand acres of the Canadian River Breaks north of Vega.

The Landergin ranch foreman, "Boots" Montgomery, the straw boss, "Con" Gurule (pronounced Gu-ru-lay), and one of the owners, Miss Virgina Corbin, were still living in three of the buildings that were at the North Ranch. Mr. Mansfield hired Boots and Con along with several other local cowboys to help in getting his cattle onto the ranch.

He began to ship his cattle to Vega by rail. It was obvious that the cattle had been on very poor range. They were very thin and weak. Several would be dead on each train load when they arrived in Vega, and several more would usually be lost on the drive of approximately fifteen miles to the ranch.

Boots Montgomery was in charge of handling the cattle (and the cowboys) from the stockyards in Vega until they were in the various pastures on the ranch.

I was thrilled when Boots hired Jack Graham and me to help. I was to be primarily the horse wrangler, but I also was to help in unloading the cattle from the trains and driving them to the first camp, which was in a small pasture about four miles north of Vega.

The rest of the way to the ranch, I drove the horses while the other men drove the cattle. The horses used in an operation such as this are known as the "remuda." In this case, the remuda consisted of about seventy horses. They were the old Landergin horses. Boots and Con knew every one of them well and by name.

I was thrilled to be working with some of the cowboys I had admired for years as I was growing up. These included Buford (Boots) Montgomery, Condito (Con) Gurule, Henry (Hank) Ruhl, Jack Johnson, and "Chic" Hargrove.

After trailing several trainloads from Vega to the ranch, Mr. Mansfield's ranch foreman, some of his cowboys, and his horses from south Texas arrived with the last trainload of cattle. After we got these to the ranch, the move was complete, and Mansfield let all of the local men go.

The Landergin brothers' heirs still controlled part of the land holdings, a few cattle, and all of the Landergin Ranch horses. Con Gurule and his wife moved to a house still owned by the Landergin heirs about two miles west of Vega. He was put in charge of their remaining holdings near Vega. Con hired Jack Graham and me to work with him. We stayed in a small bunk house behind the main house. I worked there until August, 1939.

After that I worked on various farms and cattle ranches in the area until February of 1941.

The military draft had been in effect for a while, and several of my friends had enlisted in the U.S. Army or National Guard by the time of my twenty-first birthday in December of 1940. After I turned twenty-one, I was required to register for the draft within a given period of time. Jim Bales and I began to talk about enlisting. Jim was only nineteen at the time, but he decided he wanted to go ahead and enlist so we could choose the branch of service and where we would serve, depending on openings, of course.

We decided to join the Marines, but Jim was rejected by the Marine recruiting sergeant on the spot, because of a large burn scar on the calf of his right leg. The Army recruiting office was next door to the Marine office, so the recruiting sergeant came into the Marine office to observe. When the Marine sergeant rejected Jim, the army sergeant said he believed the Army would take him.

We both then went into the Army recruiting office. The sergeant gave us the usual screening tests, and we both passed. Since Jim was under twenty-one, he had to get one of his parents to sign a form before he could be sent overseas. At that time, the Army had openings in the field artillery at Fort Sill, Oklahoma, the coast artillery in the Philippines, and the infantry in the Philippines. We decided we would like to get some travel at government expense, so we signed up for the 60th Coast Artillery, an anti-aircraft regiment stationed on Corregidor in the Philippine Islands. The sergeant gave Jim a form for parental consent. He talked his mother into signing it. She and I both lived to regret that act.

We went back to Amarillo the next day and completed signing up. We were sent to Lubbock, Texas, by train for our physical exams and inductions. We were both inducted into the U.S. Army for a three-year hitch on February 12, 1941. There were five other men inducted for service in the Philippine Islands that day at the Lubbock recruiting station, and we shipped out by train the same day for Fort McDowell on Angel Island, California, in San Francisco Bay. We arrived there the next day. Of the seven who were inducted in Lubbock that day for service in the Philippine Islands, one deserted from Angel Island, and of the six who were sent to the Philippines, two of us made it back to the states; I am the sole survivor at this time.

We got our first taste of Army life on Angel Island. We were there until March 31, 1941, and went on about three one-day passes to San Francisco. Our pay was twenty-one dollars per month, but since we were there on temporary assignment, we were only given partial pay of ten dollars at one time. I think I got two ten dollar payments during the one and one-half months I was on the Island.

Since we were what the Army calls "casuals" (in effect, soldiers awaiting shipment to new assignment) we had no drills or regular duties. The one duty we had that was really tough was K.P. (Kitchen Police). I had K.P. duty twice in the approximately six weeks I was there. All of the old Army hands agreed it was the toughest K.P. anywhere in the Army. We reported to the mess hall at two o'clock in the morning and were not released until about ten o'clock at night. We were allowed three fifteen-minute breaks during that time to go outside and smoke a cigarette. The reason for the long hours was because meals were served family style at that time. The mess hall would seat about two thousand men, but then there were almost six thousand to be fed, so we had three sittings for each meal. The K.P.s set and waited on the tables. After each sitting, the dishes were washed, and the floor was mopped. After each meal (three sittings) the floor was scrubbed with hot soapy water. If one of the K.P.s broke a dish, the cost of the dish, or dishes, was deducted from his pay.

Needless to say, the kitchen and equipment for this type of operation were huge. There was a mixing/mashing machine that would best be described as a large Mixmaster. It was about seven feet tall. The bowl must have held at least 30 gallons. I was standing near it when a couple of K.P.s carried a big kettle with at least fifty pounds of boiled potatoes in it and dumped them into the machine bowl. The cook who was in charge of the potatoes said to one of the K.P.s, "Go get me six pounds of butter." That was the amount of butter he used to butter that batch of potatoes.

The sailing list for the Philippine Islands was posted about the middle of March, and Jim and I were both on it. We were to sail from the Fort Mason docks in San Francisco on April 1, 1941, aboard the U.S. Army transport *Republic*. (It appears the April 1st sailing date was appropriate for us, considering the way it turned out.)

There were approximately five thousand men on the sailing list, as I recall. I remember a young man from Oklahoma whose name was Byrum was sitting on his bunk the day after the sailing list was posted, and he was looking pretty glum. Jim and I went to him and I asked what was bothering him. He said he was worried that the ship was going to sink. I asked him why and he said, "With that many men on it, it's bound to sink." Jim said, "Well, you can swim, can't you?" Byrum said "Yes, but . . ." Whereupon Jim interrupted him and said, "Then what the hell are you worrying about?" That broke up the conversation. That example is pretty typical of Jim Bales' humor. He was a lot of fun to be around.

We were taken off Angel Island onto harbor craft on March 31, 1941, brought to a dock at Fort Mason, and loaded into the *Republic*. We boarded the ship alphabetically, and as we went aboard, each man answered with his serial number when his name was called.

The *Republic* was a large ship, but it was old. It had been built prior to World War I, and, at one time, was one of the President Line ships. I believe at one time it was named *President Lincoln*. It still had some nice fixtures in the portion that had been the first class section.

As it turned out, Jim was assigned to a stateroom with one other man, and I was assigned to a squad room at just about the water line. There were about one hundred men assigned to this room, and the bunks were double-decked.

We sailed out of San Francisco Bay on April 1. It was a cloudy and rather windy day, and as we moved out toward the Golden Gate Bridge, the ship was gliding smoothly along, and all of us landlubbers were saying that the ship was so large that the waves couldn't toss it around much.

About the time we got to the Bridge, Jim and I were standing at the rail on the second deck of the superstructure when I looked down and saw a man come out of a passageway and lie down on a hatch cover on the main deck. He was obviously dizzy, and it soon became apparent that he was nauseated. I said to Jim, "I wonder if that guy is sea sick; it doesn't seem like it's time for that."

The sea really got choppy after we got out into the Pacific. Soon a little schooner pulled up close to our ship and lowered a lifeboat with two men in it. Our ship came to a stop and they rowed over and picked up the pilot from our ship. I marvelled at their seamanship as the pilot scrambled down a Jacob's ladder into the rowboat and they rowed over beside the schooner. As a wave brought the rowboat up about even with the deck, the pilot jumped from the row boat onto the schooner. As our ship started moving again, they blew a loud blast from the ship's whistle to salute the pilot as we pulled away. Jim grabbed me and said, "What's that?" I told him they were just blowing a good-bye whistle to the pilot. He said, "I was afraid it meant 'man the lifeboats.'"

I went down to the nearest latrine on the main deck and discovered seasickness had become an epidemic. I got out as soon as I could and went up to fresh air before I got sick. I soon discovered that if I watched the bow or the stern of the ship, the constant bobbing up and down made me start to get dizzy—a prelude to seasickness. I discovered that if I stayed amidship and looked at the horizon in a direction perpendicular to the ship, the horizon was steady and the dizziness abated.

Jim and I plus some more new-found friends decided we would not go to the mess hall due to the conditions which we found out from others who had been there. We had heard from someone that eating soda crackers and lemon drops would help prevent seasickness, so we decided to get some from the small canteen on the main deck. Jim volunteered to go get them, so we gave him the money. After a while I saw him coming up the ladder with his overcoat draped over his shoulders and looking pretty pale. When he saw me, he smiled weakly and said, "I'm ocean sick." He came on to where our group was and said, "Hell, sea sick wouldn't start it—I'm ocean sick. I was standing in line to get the crackers and lemon drops when it hit me, so I ran to the rail and puked for thirty minutes; no quarter asked, and none given."

We all got our own snacks from the canteen after that, and soon Jim began to feel better. About 9:00 PM I got a little seasick.

After that we went to bed. Neither Jim nor I were seasick after that. However, we stayed out of the mess hall for all the next day.

The next morning the captain of the ship came striding along the main deck, and one of the men asked him what was the best way to keep from getting seasick. The captain had a ready answer, "Stay on land."

Things were pretty uneventful after that. Almost everyone soon got over seasickness and began to enjoy the trip. However, there was one man who could keep nothing on his stomach for the seven days it took us to get to Honolulu, so they put him off the ship there. They probably assigned him to a unit at Schofield Barracks.

We were docked at a pier in Honolulu all day, but none of us were allowed off the ship. They did bring a troop of hula dancers on board to entertain us part of the time.

While we were docked at Honolulu, I noticed that Jim became quite moody, which was unusual for him. After I urged him to tell me what was the matter, he said he had a feeling he would never see home again. I tried to reassure him, and although he got over being moody, for the rest of the time when we were together and I mentioned something I, or we, would do when we got home, he would always say, "You mean if we get home." He had that premonition, and sure enough, he did not make it back home.

We arrived in Manila on April 22, 1941. About a dozen P-35 fighter planes buzzed the ship as a salute when we pulled into the harbor. They were the newest fighter planes there at that time. We were the first contingent of a planned massive build-up of our armed forces on the Philippine Islands. All of this group was assigned to units already there to bring them up to war-time strength. Those of us who were assigned to the 59th and 60th Coast Artillery regiments were taken immediately to Fort Mills on the island of Corregidor at the entrance to Manila Bay. Those of us assigned to the 60th Coast Artillery (AA) regiment were billeted in a concrete barracks at Middleside that had been vacated by the 92nd Coast Artillery of the Philippine Scouts in order to make room for us. We were placed on quarantine in this barracks for six weeks until we completed our basic training.

We had arrived at the hottest time of the year, so the basic training was pretty hard on us at times. Several men passed out from the heat at various times when we were standing at attention doing the manual of arms after having done close order drill for a couple of hours.

Due to the heat, our basic training was not as strenuous as it was here in the States. We did not have to run obstacle courses or do much bayonet practice. After our basic training was completed, we were assigned to the various batteries of the 60th, and a new battalion was formed. It consisted of four batteries designated as I, K, L, and M plus a headquarters battery. I was assigned to I Battery. It was an anti-aircraft machine gun battalion. We were armed with 50-caliber anti-aircraft machine guns. Our personal weapon was the 1903 Springfield rifle. We rearranged the battery letter designation and referred to ourselves as the MILK Battalion.

Our duty before the war started was not bad, and Corregidor was an exceptionally clean place for the tropics. Although our pay was only twenty-one dollars per month for the first four months and thirty dollars per month thereafter, everything was cheap compared to the states. We were paid in Philippine Commonwealth pesos which were backed by the U.S. government. Each peso was worth fifty cents.

As examples of prices, we could order cigarettes by the carton through our supply sergeant for one peso per carton. This amounted to a nickel per pack. San Miguel beer, which was brewed in Manila, was ten centavos (five cents) per bottle. Each of us contributed twenty-five centavos per month to hire Filipinos to do all of the work in the mess hall, so we did not have to do K.P.

A Filipino was assigned to each squad room, and for three pesos per month, he would make your bunk each morning and keep your shoes shined. Before anyone starts raising accusations of "exploitation," as I have heard, I wish to point out that if a Filipino received the three pesos per month from as many as twenty men, he made as much money as we did, and it was considered to be a good job by their standards. Most of them had more than twenty men paying them three pesos per month for their service.

When we first arrived on Corregidor, which everyone called "The Rock," there were several small barrios (villages) where Filipino families lived. They were mostly the families of the Philippine Scouts who were stationed there. There were two regiments of Philippine Scouts, the 91st and 92nd Coast Artillery regiments. The largest was barrio San Jose, which was located at Bottomside, near the docks.

There was a civil prison on Corregidor. Philippine Scouts were the prison guards. The prisoners did all of the maintenance work on the roads and buildings. They also hauled the trash and garbage using mule-drawn wagons. There was a detail that went around putting oil on all stagnant pools to keep down mosquitoes. As a result, Corregidor was a healthy and pleasant place to live. We didn't use mosquito bars (nets) in the barracks, and the climate was cooler than in Manila due to the sea breezes. Considering every-thing, it was a good place to serve as a soldier before the war. Due to the low pay, I was able to save enough money to take only one three-day pass to Manila before the war. I was all primed to go again when the attack on Pearl Harbor changed my plans.

Shortly after we arrived on Corregidor, the government ordered that all civilians except those employed by the Army be evacuated from the island. Within two or three months, they had been evacuated, and their homes demolished.

When I arrived in the Philippines, General Grunert was in command of American Army forces in the Philippines, and General MacArthur was organizing a Philippine Army. MacArthur was not on active duty with the U.S. Army. In July, 1941, he was recalled, commissioned a Lieutenant General, and placed in command of all Army forces in the Far East. General Grunert returned to the United States.

We were kept busy, when the weather permitted, digging in and preparing sand-bagged machine gun emplacements. The ship channels into Manila Bay on each side of Corregidor were mined in preparation for war, which we began to feel was inevitable. We believed the Philippine Islands would be the first place the Japanese would attack. A buildup in forces continued right up until the Japanese attack.

About December 1, 1941, I was in a group assigned to routine alert duty at our position on Morrison Hill on Corregidor. At this position, two fifty-caliber anti-aircraft machine guns were mounted on steel towers at tree-top level. These were old installations that had been in place a long time. Two gun crews plus a sergeant and a corporal were assigned this alert duty for two weeks at a time. We slept in tents, and at least one man was at each gun twenty-four hours a day. We were on the side of Corregidor facing the Bataan peninsula, and from our gun positions on the tower we could look down on the entire southern tip of Bataan.

On the evening of December 6, some of the men in our crew received permission from Sergeant Schultz to go to a Dorothy Lamour movie which was showing in the new Middleside Cinema just a few hundred yards from our gun positions and near the bottom of Morrison Hill. I don't remember what the name of the movie was, but I remember the movie that was showing at the Topside Cinema was *Gone With the Wind*, which was the last movie I had seen as a civilian before joining the army, and the last movie shown in the Topside Cinema on Corregidor.

A short time after the men went to the movie, they came running up the hill, breathing heavily. One of them went to Sergeant Schultz and said, "What's up?" The soldier reported that they flashed on the screen at the movie, "All men in the 60th Coast Artillery report to your positions at once." About that time, the field telephone rang, and Sergeant Schultz answered. He hung up the phone, and said, "Men, this is probably it. We have orders to keep a full crew on each gun at all times. Friendly planes approaching Corregidor will fire a blue flare from a rocket pistol. Any aircraft approaching which does not give the correct signal will be fired upon." We felt then that an attack was imminent. Nothing happened that night. The next day, Lieutenant Tom Hackett came to our position. He was then placed in command of the two guns and crews. Sergeant Schultz was in command of one gun, and Corporal Finnegan was in command of the gun I was on. The barracks were vacated, and all of the guns were set up at their prepared positions.

Nothing happened on December 7th, but we remained on war alert. (We were across the international date line. Pearl Harbor Day was December 8th over there.)

In preparation for battle communications, our batteries were given names. Before, the batteries of the 60th Coast Artillery were just letter designations—e.g., A, B, C, etc. To avoid possible confusion during radio or telephone communication they were named Albany, Boston, Chicago, Denver, Erie, Flint, Globe, Hartford, Indiana, Kingston, Lansing, and Mobile. The battery I was in—I Battery—was the only one with a state name. All the others were names of cities. I was told that the reason for this was that the officers assigning names could think of only one major city in the U.S. with a name beginning with "I." That city was Indianapolis, but they decided that was too long, so they shortened it to Indiana.

Our machine guns on Morrison Hill were located near the four three-inch anti-aircraft guns of Chicago battery. We were assigned to the Chicago battery field kitchen after the barracks were evacuated.

When we got up to go to breakfast on the morning of December 8th, it was still dark. Someone who had a radio came to where we were sitting and said the Japanese had attacked Pearl Harbor. We didn't believe it. After breakfast we went back to our position and listened to the radio which was in the shack at our command post. Don Bell was broadcasting the news over the radio station in Manila. He confirmed the attack on Pearl Harbor. He gave the latest communiqué from General MacArthur's headquarters. I remember clearly that he reported a flight of our bombers on patrol had sighted a Japanese convoy of approximately eighty transports north of Luzon and headed for the Philippines. He said the flight commander requested permission to bomb the convoy, but was told to wait for an *overt* act of war. Bear in mind that this was *after* the attack on Pearl Harbor. The planes returned to Clark Field and landed. They were almost immediately destroyed on the ground by Japanese bombers. It was almost as if the Japanese planes followed ours in. Neither General MacArthur nor the air commander, General Brereton, ever adequately explained this gross error as far as I know.

About noon, it came over our telephone that the Japanese were bombing Clark Field, so we should be extremely alert. I heard later from people who were there that the American pilots had landed their planes, parked them neatly and were inside eating lunch when bombs started falling without any warning. That is also hard to explain—not only would it indicate a lack of alertness on the part of air-warning people at Clark Field, but the Japanese had bombed Camp John Hay to the north of Clark Field before they hit Clark. It was a mess. No planes came near Corregidor that day.

Early the next morning, we could hear the bombing when they bombed Nichols Field, Nielson Field and Cavite Naval Base, all near Manila. For several days I watched the bombing of Manila Port area, Cavite Naval Base and ships in Manila Bay.

We were expecting them to bomb Corregidor at any time. Several days before Corregidor was actually bombed, a flight of heavy bombers came from over Manila Bay and passed almost directly over the north channel between Corregidor and Bataan. "C" battery as well as other batteries on Corregidor fired at them, but there was no apparent damage. All planes continued on course. We even fired at them with our machine guns. To illustrate how green we were, when the first anti-aircraft shell exploded, it went off right beneath one of the bombers. I thought it was a bomb coming toward me. A few seconds later, the black object began to expand irregularly and I realized it was smoke. I felt very foolish and told no one what I thought.

One day as the Japanese were bombing Manila Port area, Cavite naval base, Nichols Field, and ships in Manila Bay some of us were watching from our gun towers. A destroyer was out in the open bay, and a flight of three heavy bombers started trying to bomb it. They would level off and get in position to drop their bombs. It was obvious that someone on the destroyer was watching and could see when the bombs were dropped. The destroyer would make a hard turn, and the bombs would miss by several hundred yards. However, on one run, the observer apparently did not see when the bombs dropped. Maybe the sun was in his eyes. Anyway, the destroyer did not turn, and when the bombs hit, the destroyer disappeared in a big spray of water. We thought it had surely been hit but it surged from the spray full speed ahead. Apparently, it was not hit, so the bombs must have exploded between it and us. A loud cheer went up from our barracks at Middleside. It was from the Fourth Marines, who had just been moved onto The Rock and billeted in our barracks. They had not yet been deployed to their defensive positions.

Corregidor was not actually bombed until December 29, 1941, and they hit us with all they had, I think. They bombed all day long with heavy bombers, medium bombers and dive bombers. Our machine gun was chattering pretty steadily during the early hours of the attack and then only high-flying bombers continued the attack. After that day, we were not attacked by dive bombers again, until near the end after many of our guns were knocked out. I have been told, and I believe, that we inflicted such a heavy toll on the dive bombers that day, that they decided not to attack with low-flying planes again. There were many machine guns on Corregidor at that time.

At first, our three-inch A.A. guns had only twenty-one second powder train fuses. At the maximum setting, the range was only about twenty thousand feet. The Japanese continued to bomb with high-flying bombers. Sometimes they were so high our guns couldn't fire at them because they were beyond range. Then a submarine came in and brought some anti-aircraft ammunition with thirty-one second mechanical fuses. There was only enough of this ammunition to equip two batteries. Chicago "C" battery was one that got the new ammunition. Needless to say, the men of "C" battery were elated. The Japanese continued to bomb, but they were within the extreme range of the two batteries equipped with the new ammunition. They flew so high that the guns could not fire until the planes were so near over head that they would have already dropped their bombs before the gunfire reached them.

Pretty early in the war, Lt. Hackett got permission from the battery commander, and ordered us to move our machine guns down from the towers and prepare positions on the ground. After a while, Captain Godfrey R. Ames of "C" battery gave permission for us to move the gun I was on into a position which was well-prepared by the men of "C" battery for their machine gun. Later on, the gun crew of the "C" battery gun put their gun on the same tower we had moved from. As it turned out, we just swapped positions.

A short time after this, Lt. Hackett was transferred to Mobile "M" battery out on the small end of Corregidor near Kindley Field. Another lieutenant was transferred into his place, but he was not a good officer. Due to some of his cowardly actions, he was soon transferred, and Lieutenant Augustine S. Apra, who was new to our battery, was transferred to our positions. He had been stationed on Fort Wint in Subic Bay, and was evacuated to Corregidor when they were ordered to abandon it. He was one of the best and bravest officers I ever knew. He stayed with us to the end.

During this time, we on the machine guns could only watch the action and remain alert for dive bombers. I observed several planes that were hit and on fire as they left, but I never saw one actually hit the water or crash on land until about the end of March, 1942. For some reason, three planes came in below twenty thousand feet, and every three-inch battery on the "Rock" shot at them. All three planes were shot down, and one had about half of the right wing blown off. It went into a vertical dive right over the Channel between Bataan and Corregidor. From our gun positions, I saw it hit the water just offshore from Cabcaben on Bataan. I remember our lieutenant (who was in command of our two machine guns at the time) was very elated as we watched the plane fall, and he later said that it was a good morale-booster coming after all the bad news we were hearing. I agreed. Later I saw three dive bombers attack some target near Mariveles on Bataan. One of them was shot down by "G" (Globe) battery of the 60th C.A.C., which had been moved to a position near Mariveles. I saw the pilot of the plane bail out, and he hit the water approximately one mile from the shore of Bataan in the China Sea. A mosquito boat started out to pick him up, but one of the bombers that was not hit made a strafing run at the mosquito boat, and it turned back. Then the plane made a run at the downed pilot and strafed his own comrade in the water because he did not want him to be captured.

Although many bombs had hit in our area and we had very many near misses, we had lost no one in our machine gun crews when the lull came in March, 1942. During the lull, men worked preparing fox holes, digging "C" battery tunnel, and repairing "splinterproofs" around guns. During this period, General MacArthur left "The Rock" and General Wainwright assumed command.

During the latter part of March, air attacks resumed, and it seemed that they were concentrating on "C" battery. Several "sticks" of bombs hit in the "C" battery area and damaged the guns and equipment, but the men were able to make repairs rather quickly, and the battery was out of action for only short periods of time. We had some bombs hit very close to our machine gun positions, but the guns were not damaged, and no one was seriously injured.

During the first week of April, 1942, the bombing of Corregidor continued, but we could see stepped-up attacks on Bataan, and we could hear the increased intensity of artillery fire on Bataan. On the night of April 8, I could see demolitions starting on Bataan from my position on Morrison Hill. The two twelve-inch rifles on Corregidor, batteries Smith and Hearn, began firing on Bataan, letting us know the Japanese were now within their range. The guns had fired previously on Bataan during the "battle of the points" when the Japanese attempted to establish a beach head behind the lines. On the night of April 8, there was quite a fireworks display as dynamited ammunition went up. In the early morning hours of April 9, I was on the telephone duty in our machine gun pit and watching the activity on Bataan (explosions), when I noticed the handles of the ammunition chest on the machine gun began to rattle. The intensity increased, and the ground began to shake violently. Then I realized it was an earthquake. (Even the earth shuddered the night Bataan fell.)

The next morning, Captain Ames, the battery commander of "C" battery, called all the men together. The essence of his talk was that the situation was critical. From then on, we could expect heavy shelling and would take casualties. If planes were overhead at the same time we were being shelled, we were to continue firing until the cease fire was given, and then we would take care of casualties. He wound it up by saying, "If the Japs want our little hill, they will bloody well have to come and take it."

We started receiving shell fire the next day. Corregidor's gun batteries delayed counter fire for two days to give the Japanese time to get all Americans out of the area (this was the beginning of the Bataan Death March). I discovered later that, unfortunately, not all Americans were taken out of the area in time to escape our shelling. From this time on, it was sheer hell on Morrison Hill. We were under almost constant shelling and regular bombing every day, although it was not continuous at any one location. We soon learned to tell from the sound of a gun whether it was aimed in our direction or not. Therefore, we could take care of what needed to be done and only "hit the dirt" when guns fired in our direction. We had a few seconds from the time we heard the guns until the shells hit. The Japanese had guns firing at us with bore sizes all the way from 75mm to 240mm. All of their artillery remaining at the fall of Bataan was trained on Corregidor. Although the counter fire from our guns on Corregidor knocked out many of their guns, all installations on Corregidor were being systematically destroyed by constant bombing and shelling. None of the guns in positions facing the China Sea to the west of Manila Bay or to the south could fire on Bataan. They were built to fire on enemy ships at sea. We got some help from the guns on Fort Hughes.

On April 28, it seemed that every gun they had began firing on Corregidor at the same time. A terrific barrage fell upon our positions on Morrison Hill. What trees were left in the area were knocked over by the artillery blasts and then blown into splinters. My commanding officer, Lt. Apra, and myself were slightly wounded by shell fragments. Lt. Pace of "C" battery was about ten yards from us, and he was killed by the same salvo. Lt. Apra ordered us into the "C" battery tunnel, where we stayed until the shelling ceased. An ambulance came and took Lt. Apra and me to the hospital in Malinta tunnel to get our wounds dressed. Our machine gun position was hit by several rounds, and the protecting revetment or "splinterproof" was destroyed. However, the gun itself had only minor damage, and we were able to get it back in operation.

We moved over the crest of Morrison Hill and started digging a new pit for our gun. The wound in my back hurt some when I was digging, but I took my turn in the pit. Heavy shelling started again, and we retreated to a nearby bunker which had been abandoned by third battalion headquarters of the 60th Coast Artillery. I had placed all of my belongings in a neat pile, and a shell blew it all to pieces. I was left only with the clothes I was wearing. Several shells landed on the bunker over our heads. Some were duds, and I could hear them spin on the concrete after penetrating about four feet of dirt above the concrete roof.

That night I was looking for a place to lie down and get a little sleep. I found a place where a cut made for a road provided a defilade position toward Bataan. I saw a man lying there wrapped in a blanket and another blanket was beside him. As I reached over him for the extra blanket, I put my hand on the blanket covering the man lying there and it felt extra warm. I thought, "This man must be running a fever." I lay down beside him and went to sleep. Later in the night, I was awakened by two men talking. I heard one say, "It must be this one since he is on a stretcher." They then picked the man up and carried him off. I later learned that the men were medics who had come to pick up the body of one of the men in Battery "C" who had been killed by the shelling that afternoon and was partially burned. That is why the blanket felt hot when I touched it. After they carried the man away I went back to sleep. I was exhausted. Ironically, the man was killed on the machine gun tower where my gun was when the war started.

Early the next morning, I was awakened and informed that the Japanese had landed on Corregidor out near Kindley Field. There was a big fire going near the west entrance of Malinta Tunnel where they were burning records and currency. The twelve-inch mortar at Battery Way was firing as rapidly as it could. That gun was fired until it got so hot the breech stuck and could not be opened. After that only one of the battery's four guns was left in action. About four or five days before, Battery Geary, which had eight twelve-inch mortars, was completely blown up when a Japanese shell penetrated the powder magazine.

All of our officers were gone from Morrison Hill the morning of May 6, except Lt. Fortney, who had just come to "C" Battery a few days before. First Sergeant William E. Beeman of "C" Battery told us to go to our fox holes and form a defense line around Morrison Hill. "C" Battery had previously dug fox holes for this contingency, but I had not been assigned to one of them. I had no rifle since mine had been destroyed, so I went to "C" Battery magazine with Corporal Carol C. "Chad" Moore of my gun crew. He found a B.A.R. (Browning Automatic Rifle), and I found some old Enfield rifles in a box. They still had Cosmoline (a heavy grease used to protect guns from rust when they are packed away) on them. I got one of them and several bandoliers of ammunition. Moore and I went down the side of the hill facing Malinta Hill and prepared a "breastworks" in a gully. I decided to test-fire the Enfield rifle. I checked the bore, and it was open, so I bolted a shell into the firing chamber, pulled the trigger, and it just clicked. I sort of panicked. I thought, "Here the Japs are coming and I have a gun that won't shoot." (Since then I have had recurring nightmares that Japanese are coming at me and my gun won't shoot.) However, I pumped another shell into the chamber, and it fired. I fired the gun two more times and it seemed OK. Moore and I settled in, expecting to make our last stand there. We had a few silver pesos in our pockets, and we buried them under some rocks to keep the Japanese from getting them. We started telling each other that this was what we had been waiting for all these months. We would meet the Japanese face-to-face with a chance to shoot back.

We began to receive terrific barrages of shell fire. I looked down the hill to my right and saw a "C" Battery soldier named Turner struggling to bring another man named Freeman up the hill to get aid, and I saw that Freeman was badly hurt. The whole right leg of his pants was blood-soaked. Freeman was a heavy man. Moore and I ran through shell fire to help.[*] Just as we got to them, Freeman started to faint from loss of blood. We grabbed him just as a shell hit very near to us, and it gave Freeman enough additional adrenaline to help us in getting him up the steep hill to a concrete enclosure covering some buried gasoline tanks. We laid him down and I could tell he was badly wounded in his intestines on the right side. We put a bandage around him to try to slow down the loss of blood. Someone brought a stretcher down from the bunker up the hill. Then the four of us carried him up to the bunker. Gibbs and Thompson decided to try to get a truck to get Freeman to a doctor. It was obvious he would die if he could not get to a surgeon. Freeman was very brave and said in his Alabama accent, "I ain't a-dying, Gibbs. Don't go through any shell fire to get help." Gibbs and Thompson found a truck near Middleside that would run. They brought it up and Freeman was loaded on it. They couldn't get to the hospital in Malinta tunnel because the Japanese had us cut off from there by that time, so they took him to an aid station in Wheeler tunnel on Topside. I understand that he died the next day.

About this time, Sergeant Beeman gave orders for us to pull back and get under cover. He said our troops had the Japanese

---

[*] Bishop's Silver Star citation specifically mentions this action.

contained and were preparing a counter attack. I went to the "C" Battery magazine, which was full of men by that time, since nearly all the ammunition had been fired. Lt. Fortney was there, and there was a telephone still connected to regimental headquarters in Malinta tunnel. After a short time, the orders came over the telephone to demolish equipment—that we were surrendering, but to remain under cover because the Japanese would continue firing until 11:00 AM. I looked at Lt. Fortney and tears were running down his cheeks. I felt a big lump in my throat. We went out and destroyed our equipment. Since the Japanese were continuing to shell, my machine gun crew decided to go to Middleside tunnel, and later, "C" Battery men came to Middleside tunnel too. It was full of men. The floor near the entrance was covered with belted 50-caliber machine gun ammunition that the Marines stationed there had pulled out of the ammunitions chests for their 50-caliber infantry-mounted machine guns.

I don't know how my battery commander knew we were there, but he called Middleside tunnel and got me on the phone. He told me to tell the "I" Battery men to come to battery Wheeler after the bombing and shelling stopped. The Japanese continued to bomb and shell Topside intermittently until dark. The men of "I" Battery then walked up to Battery Wheeler and slept on the ground there that night. The next morning we had a battery reunion since many of us had not seen each other since the first of December. Then we fell in and Captain Shiley, the battery commander, led us to meet the Japanese and surrender. This was on the morning of May 7, 1942.

We were marching down the road, and as we rounded the end of Middleside barracks I saw a Japanese machine gun across the road on the edge of the Middleside parade ground. The Japanese behind the gun had it aimed at us, and another with his head bandaged was lying beside the machine gun. We continued to march down the road toward Bottomside. From Middleside to Bottomside, Japanese were on each side of the road about every ten yards apart. They were standing with rifles and fixed bayonets at the order-arms position (butt on ground and rifle vertical). It looked very strange because the end of the bayonet was over a foot above their heads. I am six feet, two inches tall, and when I was in the same position with my rifle and bayonet, the end of the bayonet was just below my shoulder.

We marched on down the hill to the area near the west entrance to Malinta tunnel, where it was just a huge, milling crowd.

Later in the morning, General Wainwright came out of the tunnel with some Japanese officers. They were going to the surrender site at Bottomside to sign the surrender documents. All of us who were where we could see him came to attention and saluted General Wainwright, and he started crying. Thus started our years of hell as prisoners of the Japanese.

Later that day, we were marched around Malinta Hill on the south side via the South Shore Road. I noticed a Japanese tank near the south dock. Its shape reminded me of a turtle. We went around the hill and the road passed near the east entrance to Malinta Tunnel. Down in a sort of ravine just off the road, I spotted five or six bodies in mattress covers. They were men who had died in the hospital laterals, and were carried out there. I got my first smell of decaying human flesh. After a few steps, we got into the area where the last infantry fighting took place, and dead bodies became increasingly numerous. After we had gone a few hundred yards, we passed the place there the soldier had died sitting behind his machine gun with one hand in the air. This was the scene that was the inspiration for the poem "The Unknown Soldier."

We marched on down to the 92nd garage area on the south shore out in the Kindley Field area of Corregidor. The Americans and Filipinos were segregated. We Americans were mostly on a large concrete slab in front of the 92nd garage. (Ninety-Second refers to the 92nd regiment of the Philippine Scouts. It was a Coast Artillery Regiment.) We were crowded very close together. We had no food or water, except what we had carried with us. I had picked up an abandoned mess kit in Malinta Tunnel after the surrender, but I had no canteen for water. I came upon Jim Bales, and was very relieved to see that he had survived. He was stationed near the area where the Japs landed, and had picked up an extra canteen on the battlefield, so he gave it to me. It proved to be a lifesaver more than once. Fortunately, someone discovered a water well in front of the 92nd garage. One of the medical officers had some chlorine powder, which he dropped into it,, and someone found a five-gallon can and a rope, so we started drawing water from the well. The hot sun was terrible on the concrete slab, so we started getting sticks and rigging up shades using blankets or shelter halves. Fortunately, I found some members of my battery who were camped together. They had a five-gallon wooden keg, which had been filled with water. They invited me to join them, and I gladly accepted. For a day or two, we were able to slip out a few at a time and forage some canned goods and flour from a nearby field kitchen. It was like a hobo jungle, but we managed to have sufficient water and a reasonable amount of food for the sixteen days we were held in the area. The sanitation facilities were, of course, inadequate, and the place was very filthy by the time we left. Fortunately, we could bathe on the beach and the saltwater seemed to help the wound on my back, which had festered some. It was pretty well healed by the time we left.

I will relate one more strange thing that happened there, and then I will spare you further grisly details on Corregidor. Although many men were there, I have never seen this incident mentioned in writing. Of course, most of the men probably never knew exactly what happened.

I think it was the next day after we were concentrated in the 92nd garage area that a thirty-caliber machine gun commenced firing on a knoll just to the north. I estimate it fired about thirty rounds and stopped. Fortunately, the gun was not pointed in the direction of the mass of men in our area. My first thought was that the hot sun had cooked off the round in the chamber and started the gun firing. If I had stopped to think, I would have realized it would only have fired one shot in that case because something had to keep the trigger depressed to make it fire continuously.

We Americans did not get excited about it, but the Japanese guards on our perimeter hit the dirt and prepared to move up the hill toward the machine gun. One of the guards motioned to some of the American soldiers to come up to where he was. I was close enough to observe everything, but not quite close enough to be called upon for shield duty. The Japanese guards had four or five Americans walk in front of them up the hill.

After a while the Americans came back, and told those of us nearby that a dead soldier had actually fired the gun. He had died with his finger still through the trigger guard, but when his hand relaxed, the gun stopped firing. Then as decomposition set in, and his body swelled, the finger swelled enough to depress the trigger, and the gun fired all the ammunition left in the belt.

The first rain of the rainy season came on the evening of May 22. We received orders to move out the next morning. They did not move us because of the rain. It was just coincidental that we were moved the next day.

On the morning of May 23, we were loaded onto ships off the south dock of Corregidor. We were hauled out to the ships in barges and got aboard by ladder. We slept on the deck overnight and the ships headed for Manila early the next morning. The Filipinos were taken to the dock in Manila and unloaded. I am not sure to what prison camp they were sent. The ships loaded with Americans headed out toward Paranaque Beach.

This was out near the end of Dewey Boulevard. We were loaded from the ships onto Japanese landing barges, and taken to the beach where we disembarked in the water about four feet deep. We waded ashore and were lined up on Dewey Boulevard along which were many beautiful homes and some nice hotels. The Japanese had rousted out the Philippine people to line the boulevard along the route. They were supposed to witness the conquered Americans and their Japanese captors. I shall never forget the look on the face of an older Filipina. She had a handkerchief over her mouth, but I could see the tears running down her cheeks, and the sheer agony showed on her face. Many of the Filipinos surreptitiously gave a "V-for-victory" sign. I think the march backfired and had the opposite effect to what the Japanese expected.

We marched on past the Manila Hotel, which had been made into a Japanese headquarters for the higher brass. There were many small one-man tanks lined up in front of the hotel. We marched on down into downtown Manila to the old Bilibid prison where we spent the night in the prison yard. We were given a rice ball and a cup of onion soup that night (May 24). We stayed there on May 25th, and on the morning of May 26th most of us were marched to the train station and loaded into steel freight cars. There were one hundred men in each narrow gauge car. It was very hot and crowded. Fortunately, our guard on the car left the door open pretty wide so we could get air. I was where I could look out the door, and I could see Filipino children along the track; and as we passed they would give us the "V" sign. We rode most of the day, and then unloaded in the town of Cabanatuan. We were marched to a school house with a large fenced yard where we spent the night. Early the next morning we moved out and marched approximately twenty miles to Cabanatuan Prison Camp No. Three.

This prison camp, as well as Cabanatuan No. One and Camp O'Donnell, were camps that were hastily constructed just before the war by the Philippine Commonwealth government as training camps for the Philippine Army.

The barracks were constructed with a frame of wood, sides of woven strips of bamboo and roofs of nipa thatch. The bunk bays were split bamboo, and were double-decked. Some of the headquarters buildings and officers' quarters were constructed entirely of wood.

As we arrived in Camp No. Three, we were assigned to barracks, with about 100 men to each barracks. I was originally assigned to a barracks near the main gate, but a few days later I was moved to another barracks. The rainy season had begun, and the amount of rain that fell each day steadily increased.

We had only been in camp about two weeks, I think, when I heard that four men had wandered out into the road between the American side of the camp and the Japanese side. The gate was never locked, and guards were not posted at this gate, but were posted in the road on the perimeter of the camp. Actually, American medics were allowed to cross back and forth across the road because the so-called hospital was across the road and on the Japanese side.

The Japanese saw the four soldiers out in the road, so a guard went to them and ordered them back into camp where they were tied to posts and accused of attempted escape. They were beaten, off and on, for a couple of days while they were tied up in the hot sun.

I understand that the orders came from the Japanese headquarters in Manila to execute them. Four shallow graves were dug about two feet deep within the prison compound and just across a draw from the barracks I was in. I witnessed it all when the Japanese firing squad marched the men through the camp to the grave sites. The men were made to stand in the shallow graves, and the firing squad executed them following the usual ritual.

This probably had the effect the Japanese intended because it made all of us have second thoughts about trying to escape. Later, we were divided into ten-man squads and told that if one of the ten escaped, the other nine would be shot. This was designed to make us watch each other. There were occasions when this was carried out. There were numerous other executions, but I only witnessed one other, and it was one man wrongly accused of trying to escape.

We soon began to develop skin ulcers, and various diseases such as dengue fever, malaria, and dysentery. We also were soon affected with malnutrition diseases such as beri-beri, scurvy, and pellagra.

In addition to regular malaria, there were several cases of what the doctors called "cerebral malaria." It would come on suddenly with a high fever, and the victim immediately became delirious. The fever would usually break within ten days to two weeks if the victim did not die first. More men died than got over it.

From my notes, it was about August 23, 1942, when Jim Bales, who was not in the same barracks as I was, came over to my barracks and said he had made arrangements to borrow a five-gallon can, and if I wanted to, he would bring it over to my barracks the next day. We could fill it and find a good spot where we could both take a bath. I would pour water on him with a canteen cup, and he would soap his body. Then I would pour water for him to rinse off, and he would then do the same for me. I told him I would be grateful if he would.

The next day, August 24, right after our noon meal, I went out and got in line to fill my canteen from a spigot near my barracks. We only had one spigot for each row of barracks, which amounted to about one for 300 or more men.

While I was standing in line in the hot sun, I began to feel woozy. I left the line and went back to my barracks. My blanket was in an upper bay, and when I started to climb up, my knees collapsed. A couple of the men helped me up to my bunk, and I was lying there when Jim came to keep our arrangements for a bath. I raised my head and told him I didn't feel like it. He looked at me, and I could tell he was concerned. He left, and that is the last thing I remember except for a few incidents for about two weeks when I came to my senses in the "hospital."

Cerebral malaria had hit me. I was lucky in that the Japanese had given our doctors a supply of quinine about that time. One thing I can remember is First Sergeant Damon waking me up during the night to give me quinine. Sgt. Damon was the non-commissioned officer in charge of the barracks, and Lieutenant Lackey was the officer in charge.

One day I heard someone say, "We came for McKendree." It sort of made me aware when I heard my name. Sgt. Damon called to me, and I went to the front of the barracks. It shook me up when I saw the medics with a stretcher, because I knew they had come to take me to the "hospital," which was mostly where they took men to die. Sgt. Damon wrote my name and serial number on a slip of paper and put it in my shirt pocket. They carried me to the hospital, and I only remember one thing that happened before my fever broke. One day a medic brought me two or three bananas and said my buddy "Chad" Moore had sent them to me. Chad was on my machine gun crew, and we became quite close during the siege of Corregidor. We were together the entire time from December 1, 1941, to May 7, 1942.

After my fever broke, and I regained consciousness, I began to feel OK. After about a week, they sent me back to my barracks on or about September 10, 1942.

Everyone was glad to see me, especially Jim Bales and Chad Moore. They all said they never expected to see me again when they carried me away. Lt. Lackey told me what happened at the barracks while I was out of my mind. At the time I got sick, the doctors had a schedule when a doctor would come to each barracks and check men who were developing malnutrition diseases. They had some canned food they would give to men they thought would be helped most. Of course, it was a very limited amount.

On the day I got sick, Lt. Lackey told me to get in line outside with the men lined up for the doctor. He said I got in line, and sat down on the ground. When the doctor got to me, he said "What's the matter with you?." I said, "Don't mind me, I'm just watching the ball game." The doctor said, "What?" I said, "I don't live here, I'm just watching the ball game." Whereupon the doctor told Lt. Lackey to bring me to his office.

When I got there, Lt. Lackey said the doctor asked me several questions, and I gave weird answers. He asked me if I knew Lt. Lackey; I looked at the Lieutenant and said, "I have seen him somewhere before." He took my temperature, of course, and immediately put me on quinine. Lt. Lackey said they assigned a man to watch me at all times. I would get up and go to the latrine, get my meals, etc. The only thing was, I was out of my mind, and they were afraid I might try to go through the fence and get shot.

After I got back from the hospital, the doctor who initially examined me had me come to his office weekly for some time. I think he could hardly believe I was still breathing. Once in his office, I stole a look at his notes for my first visit. He had written that I stuttered and stammered my words. Did not know people who were very familiar to me. Temperature 105.6. That is all I got to read of his notes.

During this time, Sgt. Tom Melody formed a group of men to be entertainers, and they would put on a show once each week. They sang songs, told jokes (clean jokes) and performed skits. Tom Melody was a good M.C., and some of the entertainers were quite good.

Some time in October of 1942, I developed a pretty severe case of dysentery. At the same time, we were notified the camp was to be evacuated. We were all to be moved to Cabanatuan Camp No. One.

On October 20th, we were notified we would move the next day. I went to visit Jim that night, and we talked for an hour or so. When I left him, he said, "Don't let them shits get you down." Those were the last words he spoke to me.

The next day, those who were able, marched out of Camp No. Three to Cabanatuan Camp No. One, about eight miles to the west. Jim marched out, but due to my dysentery, I was among those hauled by truck. I was put in the hospital area of Camp No. One. There, I saw for the first time men who looked like skeletons with skin on them. When they would lie on their backs, their vertebrae would show in the abdominal area.

When we left Camp No. Three, sixty-nine men had died during the five months we were there, not counting the four who were executed. Now, at Camp No. One, men were dying at between forty and fifty per day, most of them in the dysentery area where I was. I am sure there had been days there when as many men died in one day (sixty-nine) as died during the five months we were at Camp No. Three. Most of the men at Cabanatuan Camp No. One were the survivors of the Death March on Bataan, and the Camp O'Donnell death camp. They were in a more weakened condition when they went into prison camp than those of us who were on Corregidor. There were several reasons for this which I will not discuss here except to say that I believe the two principal reasons were the prevalence of malaria on Bataan, which we did not have on Corregidor, and the Bataan Death March. The conditions were terrible. Almost every morning when I had to make a run for the latrine, there would be several dead men along the path who had died during the night while trying to make it to the latrine.

There were two larger wooden buildings near the barracks I was in where they carried men who could no longer care for themselves. One was called "Zero Ward" and the other "St. Peter's Ward" for obvious reasons. Very few men who were taken there lived to tell about it, but some few did.

About October 28, 1942, a large group of men were taken from the camp and shipped to Japan. Jim was in that group, and he died there about June of 1943, I think. I learned of his death in a letter I received from my parents on March 28, 1944. The letter was dated July 4, 1943.

In November of 1942, the Japanese started furnishing two or three carabao (water buffalo) about two times per week. They were butchered and divided by American personnel in the camp. Each kitchen in the camp got enough that about two or three half-inch cubes of meat would be in each cup of soup. Nothing was wasted. The blood was caught and saved by the butcher, and every edible part was saved to go into the soup. As a result, the soup was much more nutritious than the greens and water soup we had been getting. As a matter of information, in all of the prison camps, our meals consisted of an army mess kit full of watery rice gruel for breakfast (we called this lugao), a mess kit of steamed rice and about three-fourths of a canteen cup full of soup at noon, and the same thing for the third meal each day.

About the same time the Japanese increased our rations, the camp received a good amount of canned beef, dried fruit, cocoa, and vitaminized candy from the South African Red Cross. We also received some canned food, cigarettes, and tobacco from the American Red Cross.

As a result of this additional food, everyone began to feel better, and the death rate began to decline. It was at this time that we acquired can labels and other pieces of paper to write on. Men so inclined and talented enough, began to write poetry. The poetry began to be passed around and I started collecting it. Some poetry had been written before the war and during the fighting on Bataan and Corregidor. Men had carried copies of the poetry into camp and it began to surface. I copied all I could when I had the chance.

On December 15th I was pronounced fit to leave the hospital side and go to the duty side of the camp. The work performed by the men on the duty side was, for the most part, work on the prison farm which was in the process of being established and expanded. There were other work details such as the burial detail, wood detail, unloading supplies brought in by trucks and carabao carts, etc.

On Christmas Day, 1942, we received our first individual Red Cross boxes from the American Red Cross. We were eating comparatively well at this time. Just to show that the high death rate was almost entirely due to starvation, the death rate dropped dramatically, and I remember it was one day in February, 1943, that the camp celebrated the first day since the camp started that no one had died.

During this period from about March, 1943, until I left Cabanatuan Camp No. One on September 1943, I was allowed to send five post cards home. They were very limited in the amount of information I was allowed to transmit. They were mostly multiple choice things that allowed me to underline certain things to say. My family kept these post cards carefully, and they are now in the Barker Texas History Center Archives at The University of Texas in Austin, with the cement sack booklet of poems.

On September 19, 1943, I was in a group sent from Camp No. Three to Camp No. Four, which was a new camp near the town of Las Piñas, very near Manila and near Nichols Field. We were put to work building an airfield for primary trainers. It was all pick and shovel work. We were digging and filling to make a level runway.

While at this camp, I copied additional poetry. Most of it was the poetry written by Elmer Smith. He let me copy it from his originals. I also picked up the cement sack at this camp from which I later made a booklet, and recopied all the poems into it.

At Las Piñas, we each received four individual American Red Cross boxes during the period from November, 1943, through February, 1944. The boxes mostly contained food (canned meat, chocolate, some cheese and dried fruit), toilet articles (a toothbrush, sewing kit, shaving cream) and cigarettes.

All of the Old Gold brand of cigarettes were confiscated by the Japanese when they learned this was written on the package: "Freedom is our heritage. Our armed forces are engaged in a great conflict to preserve that heritage. Our freedom will be preserved if we, too, do our part to help them." It was not acceptable to keep the cigarettes and give the empty packs to the Japanese. They insisted on taking the cigarettes, too—no doubt because they wanted the American cigarettes for themselves.

I received a personal box from home in March, 1944, and I received my first letters from home on March 28, 1944. In one of these letters I learned of Jim's death, which really upset me. I received additional letters on July 31 and August 15, 1944.

On the morning of September 21, 1944, I was in camp due to a very bad abscess in my left heel as a result of a stone bruise. We worked barefoot all the time there. All of the other men who were able were at work on the airfield. It was a cloudy morning with heavy overcast. I heard a Japanese flying boat, which was similar to our old PBY patrol bombers, flying low overhead. I went out, and it flew over our camp, gaining altitude. It had just taken off from Manila Bay. I was watching it when suddenly I heard aircraft machine guns chatter, and the Japanese plane burst into flames and went down. I heard motors, and I looked up and counted fifty-six carrier planes coming out of the clouds in formation. I learned later that they were Grumman planes. They started peeling off and diving to drop bombs and make strafing runs. What really pleased me was that the Japanese were taken by surprise as we were at Clark Field. A few Japanese fighter planes got off the ground, but it did not take long for the American planes to clear them from the air. Most of their planes were destroyed on the ground.

After they took care of the Japanese planes, they started concentrating on the docks and ships in the bay. There was quite a bit of anti-aircraft fire, and I admired the nerve of our pilots as they peeled off and dived through heavy fire to drop their bombs on the targets. I observed about three or four American planes shot down. They continued the bombing for several hours, and left many fires burning. Late that night, there was a very large explosion. Apparently it was a ship that blew up in Manila Bay near the docks.

The planes returned again on September 22, but it was not as spectacular as the day before. We were all excited, thinking the Americans would soon return and we would be liberated if we managed to live through it. For the next eight days, things were pretty much as they had been before, except we felt better.

Then on September 30th, most of us were disappointed when we were told we were moving out. A few men were left in the camp. They were primarily the truck drivers and mechanics. We thought they were lucky, but as it turned out, they were not. Most of those left behind went out on other ships which were sunk. A few survived the sinkings.

On October 1, 1944, we were taken by truck to a dock in Manila. A small freighter was tied up at the docks. We could look out over Manila Bay and see many hulks and masts sticking out of the water. They were the wrecks of ships sunk by the American planes.

The Japanese also brought to the docks about 250 British prisoners from Singapore who were survivors of a prison ship loaded with British prisoners which was sunk offshore from Olongapo by American planes during that first bombing. There were about 1,200 men on that ship, and only 250 survived.

We were loaded onto a small freighter named the *Haro Maru*. I only recently learned the correct name of the ship. We dubbed it the "Benjo Maru." (*Benjo* is Japanese for latrine or feces.) We were loaded onto the ship into the two holds. We went down the temporary stairs into the hold and were lined up shoulder to shoulder and back to belly until the hold was completely full. I thought at first they were loading it that way to take us out to a larger ship in the bay. After we were loaded, they told us we were on the way to Japan and it would take about seven days. I thought, "God, how can we live like this for seven days?" We were loaded in on top of powdery coal, which was the fuel the ship used. They had hauled some horses in the hold before us, so there were 2" x 6" boards bolted to the ribs of the ship up to about eight feet above the coal. Many men took blankets or shelter halves and tied them to the 2" x 6"s to make hammocks. There were probably at least one hundred men in these hammocks. This gave the rest of us room to sit, although it was still very crowded. Fortunately, I was against the side of the ship. Usually, the steel was cooler than the air in the hold, so I got some relief when I put my forehead against the steel.

We got underway, and for several days we traveled all day, but would pull into a cove at night and drop anchor. I later was told by Curtis Stevens, Jr., who was lucky enough to have been assigned to a job on topside, and did not have to go into a hold, that it was two or three days before we actually left Manila. They would steam out of Manila Bay and form up a convoy in the China Sea. Then submarines were sighted, so they put back into Manila Bay. It was terribly hot in the holds. I remember one day the Japanese commander let us on deck, ten men at a time, but we had to crawl on our hands and knees while we were on deck. We were told not to go near the rail or throw anything over the side, and if we did we would be shot. We were traveling about four or five miles offshore at the time I was on deck. I suppose we were still offshore from Luzon. After we had been on deck and then went back to the hold, as we started down the ladder, the stench of the hold and the heat would hit, and it made one realize even more how terrible it was in the hold.

As I recall, we got one canteen of water and two meals of rice per day. Each meal consisted of about one level mess kit of steamed rice. To conserve water, I would rinse my mess kit after each meal and then drink the water I had used to rinse it. Needless to say, one canteen of water per day was not enough in the hot, stinking hold. Men began to go mad with thirst after four or five days. Men would try to steal canteens from others and get beaten over the head with the canteens they were trying to steal. Some men were beaten to death. When a man died, he was hauled up by rope the next morning and thrown over the side. Most of the terrible things happened at night. The men would tend to keep their composure during the day, but some would become mad or delirious during the night.

On about the fourth or fifth day out (I believe it was on October 7, 1944), I suddenly heard an explosion near our ship. Some burning oil sprayed onto our ship and some smoke came into the hold. Then we heard many depth charges going off. We knew the convoy was being attacked by a submarine or submarines. Everyone got excited and the temperature in the hold immediately went up by several degrees.

A short time later, a young man we called "Sammy" and several Englishmen who had been in the rear, or aft, hold, were transferred to the forward hold where we were. They said the conditions were even worse in the other hold, so the Japanese transferred some to the forward hold. Sammy was covered with "Guam blisters" (a skin condition which makes small, watery blisters, primarily around body areas which are wet with sweat). Someone had painted a good part of his body with what looked like calamine lotion. Sammy was very excited because he had seen the ship blown up, and he said it was a tanker. After we had settled down again, a sailor who was a former submariner told us that the submarine had sounded our ship three times with its sonar. The fact that we were on a small ship probably saved us from being the target of a torpedo. The sailor claimed he could hear a "ping" when the sonar sounded us. He was where he could put his ear to the side of the ship. He also said it sounded to him as if the submarine was sunk by the depth charges. However, two days later, our convoy was again attacked by submarines. According to notes I made, the submarine attacks were on October 7 and 9, 1944.

These submarine attacks created more excitement, which caused the temperature in the hold to rise, and this caused more men to go mad with thirst. By this time, my lips were cracked and my tongue was dry and cracked. However, I rationed my water so that I would drink the last sip when they called for us to send up our canteens for refill.

I think it was the next day after the last submarine attack that a Japanese destroyer delivered two men to our ship. (Sometimes in my memory it seems that there were five men, but at other times I remember it as two. I never saw any of them.) These men were tied up some place on deck where the men going to fill our canteens and to get our rice had to walk by them. Everyone was given warning that anyone who tried to talk to them would be shot. These men were survivors from another ship which was loaded with American prisoners of war. The Japanese guards on that prison ship attempted to be sure that all prisoners went down with the ship, but miraculously the two (or five) survived. They were picked up by a Japanese destroyer. I will not relate their story here, but it was a very ugly one.

On October 11, the navy chief petty officer who stood at the hold and tied the rope around each bucket of rice and lowered it into the hold for our meals said, "Men, we are pulling into a port, so we may be unloading before long." Our spirits rose, but were quickly crushed when he said, "Hell, we're not pulling into a port in Japan, this is Hong Kong." He had been there before and recognized it.

We pulled into Hong Kong harbor and dropped anchor. We stayed there until October 21. During this time, additional coal and water were brought aboard. Since the holds were loaded with prisoners, the coal was off-loaded from Chinese junks onto the deck of the ship. I don't know how it was later transferred to the boiler room.

While we were in Hong Kong, we got to go up on deck periodically. About twenty men would go up at a time and stay for about fifteen minutes. I still remember how Hong Kong looked then, and it was quite different from the way it looks now. While we were in Hong Kong, several men died and were thrown overboard into the harbor. I remember one of them was a man named Sharp from Clovis, New Mexico, whom I had been working with and made friends with at Las Piñas.

On October 14, American planes bombed Hong Kong and ships in the harbor. It was not a large air raid and was over in a short time. Machine guns on our ship fired at one of the planes, but no bombs landed close to us. We left Hong Kong on October 21, and arrived in Formosa (now Taiwan) on November 2. I assume the port was Takao, because that seemed to be the port where all of the prisoner of war ships anchored when they went to Formosa. We stayed in the harbor there on board ship until November 8th, when we unloaded. We had been on the ship thirty-nine days; the reader will remember we had been told originally that the trip would take seven days. Many men had died by that time, and we were all getting very weak. The death rate would have increased rapidly if we had stayed aboard the "Benjo Maru" very much longer. Many of the men had to crawl off the ship.

Now I will make some additional remarks about events and conditions in the hell ship. I cannot place the date when some of these things occurred, so this is a general discussion.

In regard to the sanitary conditions on the ship, the toilet facilities consisted of a five-gallon can which was lowered into the hold on a rope. The can was then passed around for the men to use to relieve themselves. As you can imagine, this one can was hardly adequate for approximately 700 men. One would hear cries from the men to "pass the honey bucket." It would be over-filled and then passed back to a certain place to be hoisted up and the contents would be thrown over the side. The procedure would start again. As the over-filled bucket was being hauled up, some of the contents would spill out, and the men below would get splashed. Due to the small amount of food and water we received, the output soon decreased, and it was not so hard to get the "honey bucket" passed to you. Especially during the first days, the men had to relieve themselves where they were, in the slack coal (powdery coal) they were lying on. One would dig down into the coal, use the depression, then cover it up. Needless to say, this contributed to the foul air and was the reason for the name "Benjo Maru." We soon became dehydrated, and as near as I can remember, and as well as I could remember at the time when I got off the ship, I did not have a bowel movement during the time I was in the hold of the ship. I urinated several times, but very little compared to normal. After I got to the new prison camp and had all the water I wanted to drink, body functions returned to normal.

At times during the voyage, men became like animals. This occurred especially at night. Men crazed with thirst would attempt to steal or forcibly take the canteens of other men. This would result in fighting, screams, and beatings, and often resulted in the death of one or another. Many times at night, there was pandemonium, usually in the central area of the hold. I did not actually witness this, but I have heard many times from different men who are reliable that there were cases when a man cut another man's jugular vein and drank his blood. (This is the only thing I have told that is hearsay to me, but I feel it should be told.) As I recall, the nights after the two submarine attacks were particularly bad due to the fact that our excitement raised the temperature so much and also led many to believe we were doomed.

I recall one night when a man I knew came running across to the place where I stood. It was a moonlit night, and I recognized him in the moonlight that was coming in between the boards covering the hold. I said, "McMahan, where are you going?" He said, "I am going up on that big high tower up there." He then took off toward the other side of the hold, walking on men as he went.

I remember another man named Barnett, who walked over to me and squeezed between me and another man. He put his arms around our necks and started talking. He slurred his words and sounded as if he were drunk. We talked for some time, and then he leaned back against the side of the ship. The next morning, he was dead.

Each morning after daylight, Captain Biedenstein, who was the senior American officer in our hold, would call out, "Everyone wake up. Shake the man next to you to see if he is dead or not. Pass the dead to the forward part of the hold." The dead would then be pulled up on a rope and thrown over the side.

I can remember one night when it was pretty quiet, I could hear a man named Smack naming cold things to eat or drink. He named ice cream, Coca-Cola, frozen Milky Ways. Then he said, "Hot dogs—no, no, *cold* dogs." I could hear men who were delirious talking about various things and to people they previously had known. Some would be talking to their folks back home.

I will now describe how we were served our rice and water.

After we were put on the ship, we were assigned numbers (I don't recall when or how they were assigned). We wrote our number on our mess kits and canteens. To receive water, we passed our canteens forward, and they were hauled up by rope to the deck where men who were assigned that good duty took them to be filled. After filling, they were lowered back into the hold. The number of each canteen was called out, and the man to whom the canteen belonged would sound off and hold up his hand until the canteen was passed to him. When the buckets of rice were lowered into the hold, our mess kits were passed forward and filled from the buckets, the number on each mess kit was called out and they were passed back in the same manner as the canteens.

We ran into a problem with the men who were moved up from the aft hold because the numbers assigned to them duplicated numbers assigned to men in the forward hold. This was solved by having them add an "A" after their number. I must give credit to three men who were instrumental in establishing what organization we had and who did nearly all the work in distributing the rice and water. They are army sergeants McNulty and Neal, and Marine Sergeant Portes. Sergeant McNulty developed jaundice during the voyage and turned very yellow. I know he didn't feel well, but he kept at it. There were many other men whose behavior was exemplary during the voyage, while others behaved like animals.

As for myself, I tried to remain as quiet as possible and move as little as possible to conserve energy and try to avoid contributing to the temperature in the hold. That is, I tried to avoid generating heat by not moving around more than absolutely necessary. I hesitate to say this, but a compliment I received from a marine who was near me during the trip is one that I appreciated more than any other compliment I have ever received. As we were unloading from the ship, he reached out his hand and shook hands with me and said, "I just want to tell you that you are one who acted like a man on this trip." I can't say what prompted him to say it, but I appreciated it very much.

There is one thing I would tell about the Japanese on the *Haro Maru*. There were 3" x 12" timbers across the hold of the ship. They were spaced about five or six inches apart to allow air in. When we were under danger of attack either from submarines or by air, they would attach cables across the hold and tighten them with a winch so that we could not get out of the hold should the ship go down.

When we unloaded from the ship onto the dock in Formosa, a Japanese soldier who had lived in the USA many years (if not all of his life) called the roll. As each prisoner's name was called, he moved to a different area on the dock. I know the Japanese who called the names and gave instructions had learned English in America because of the accent and the American slang he used.

We were divided into two groups and loaded into trains. The group I was in included many of the Englishmen. We rode on the train all night. I sat beside an Englishman, and he talked most of the night. Because of his accent and the fact that we were both half asleep, I understood very little of what he said. After we got to the prison camp on Formosa on November 9, 1944, we had enough water to clean up, and to drink all we wanted. I think the camp was near a place called Endin. We occupied the buildings of an elementary school.

When we arrived in this camp, we were issued Japanese G-string underwear, a pair of pants made with light weight material, and a pair of wrap leggings. We didn't work hard in the camp, and the guards were not brutal as they had been in the Philippines. This gave us a chance to recuperate some from the trip on the hell ship. I had time there to make the booklet from the cement sack and recopy all of the poems into it.

Formosa was beautiful and productive in the area where we were. I have often said that I saw more food, yet had so little to eat, on Formosa than anywhere else. I could look down the hill from our camp and see pineapples, papayas, and a fruit we called star-fruit (caranbola). I had never seen this fruit before. A cross-section of this fruit is in the shape of a five-pointed star. It grew abundantly on the trees, and I could see a lot of it under the trees, rotting on the ground.

One day, a guard took some of us from the camp to a nearby farm where the farmer had a large pile of rice straw under one of these trees. There was a lot of star-fruit on the ground. I went around the straw stack to where the guard couldn't see me, and started picking up fruit as fast as I could and sticking it inside the waist of my pants. It fell down the pants-leg, but the wrap legging kept it from falling out. The Japanese farmer came around the straw stack and saw me picking it up, but he did not say anything to the guard.

We all grabbed an armful of the rice straw as directed and carried it back to camp to use as bedding. Fortunately, the guard did not search us or pat us down when we went back into camp, so I smuggled the fruit into camp OK. I ate most of the fruit, but I gave two or three to my closest friends in the barracks and traded some for additional rice or soup. Anyway, I ate better for a couple of days.

Down the hill from our camp were about twelve or fifteen of the luckiest men I ever saw who were prisoners of the Japanese. The place where they were confined was apparently at one time the home of a wealthy family. It was a large two-story house with a large swimming pool. The Japanese had taken it over to be used as a hospital for some British prisoners of war. I understand that the other British prisoners were moved out, but these few men were so weak and sick that they were left behind with a British doctor to recuperate. When we arrived there, they were all very healthy, for Japanese prisoners of war, and were living a life of ease.

When we first arrived in our camp, there was no kitchen, so these British soldiers prepared our food and brought it up to us in a push cart. We appreciated them very much.

I think it was at Christmas time that these men were given permission by the Japanese to put on a show for us. They came up the hill with their gear in the push cart. They set up an impromptu stage, and put on a very good variety show, under the circumstances, with costumes, skits, songs, dancing and jokes. There was a Scotsman in the group who had somehow managed to keep his kilt with him in perfect condition. He wore it in one of the skits. Some of us went up to look at it after the show. He was very proud of it, and told us how many yards of wool material was in it, but I don't remember the amount. He carefully folded it, put it into a footlocker and locked it. I have always wondered whether or not he made it through the war with his kilt.

We saw the first American planes over Formosa on January 3, 1945. Only one flew close to us, and it flew right over our camp. They bombed again on the fourth. There was an all day bombing on January 9th. We could hear the bombs, but they were not close enough for us to see the action.

On January 11, we were issued British wool army overcoats and shoes. I assume they had been captured by the Japanese in Hong Kong and perhaps Singapore.

We left this camp on January 12, 1945, when we were put on a train and went back to the port of Takao. We boarded a ship the next day, the *Melbourne Maru*. We were loaded into the hold, but there were bays built in them, so we slept on two levels. There was enough room to lie down and to get up and walk some. Compared to the first ship, it was a luxury cruise. There were some Japanese troops on board, also. We sailed on January 14, and the first day or two out, the Japanese soldiers on board became seasick, so we were given the food they did not eat. We ate pretty well for a couple of days. According to my notes, we anchored January 17 off the coast of China. I believe we were north of Shanghai. I am not sure what gave me the idea of our location, other than the fact that I was in a work detail on deck one day, and the sea was very yellow. I assumed we were in or near the Yellow Sea. We were anchored for about twenty-four hours and got under way again on January 18th. We reached port in Japan on the night of January 23rd. We heard depth charges close by before we pulled into port. We stayed on the ship January 24th and unloaded January 25, 1945. It seemed very cold to us since we had been in the tropics over three and one half years. Some men had been in the tropics longer than that.

We stayed the night of January 25th, all day January 26th, and until the morning of January 27th in a warehouse at the docks. We were very cold, and at least one man died there. We boarded a train at 8:00 AM January 27th, and pulled into Tokyo on the 28th. The Japanese pulled the blinds on the train windows because they didn't want us to see how heavily Tokyo had been bombed. I got some glimpses of it anyway. We changed trains in a station in Tokyo.

I was very surprised to see oranges growing on trees near Tokyo in January. I thought Japan was too far north for oranges, but I suppose the Japanese current keeps part of the coastal area warm.

We rode all day the rest of January 28th, and arrived on the night of the 29th at Odati, on the far northern part of the island of Honshu. To the best of my knowledge, the name of the town was Odati, but I am not absolutely sure. It was very cold, and snow was about three feet deep. We walked to our new prison camp about a mile from town.

We were in a mining camp. The barracks were of frame construction with only one thin wall of wood siding. The roofs were made of tree bark. As I said, it was very cold, and we had no heat. There was a very small wood stove in each squad room, but we were issued only five or six sticks of cherry wood about one and one-half inches in diameter and two feet long per day. That was barely enough to heat up the stove.

Fortunately, the Japanese took some pity on us, I suppose, because they did not make us work in the mine for about three weeks. They issued each of us two comforters, but they were so short we had to sleep curled up so our feet wouldn't be out in the cold. The only way we could get warm was for two of us to bunk together. We put two comforters down to lie on, covered with the other two, plus our overcoats.

One day I was in a group of four or five men called out to unload some wood for the kitchen. We walked out the front door, and I thought I was in Alaska. There was a Japanese there with a fur cap on, heavy clothing, and a dog hide on his back with the front leg part tied around his neck and the hind leg part tied around his waist. He reminded me very much of an Eskimo. He had a horse and sleigh, and the sleigh was loaded with cherry wood which we carried to the kitchen.

On February 20th, we were all called out to begin work in the mine. They took us out and lined us up in front of the mine headquarters building. The mine superintendent gave us a speech, none of which I remember, and I thought I was going to freeze. Standing there and not moving was terrible. I got so cold that I got sick at my stomach and almost lost what little breakfast I had.

After his speech, we went to work in the mine. It was an open pit mine with several levels for people to work with picks and shovels. Little rail lines were laid, and push cars on the rails were loaded, then pushed out to the fill if they were in any of the upper levels.

The lowest level was the ore level. Cars loaded with ore were pulled up the rails by hoist to ground level and then pushed to the ore chute. There the ore was loaded into buckets which were carried up the hill to the mill by a cable which operated like a ski lift.

We were issued sandals made of rice straw which we had to wear in the mine because we slipped too easily with leather shoes. It's a wonder our feet did not get frost-bitten because our shoes and socks would get wet. Parts of the sandals and socks would have ice on them.

It was probably about the middle of March when the Japanese gave us enough wood to heat up a big wooden vat full of water so we could take a bath. The fire was under a cast iron coil, and the water circulated by thermo-siphon process until the water in the tub was heated. About ten men at a time went to the bath house and bathed. The order in which we bathed was assigned by barracks. By the time three hundred men bathed in the vat of water, it was getting pretty soupy, but it felt good to everyone to get a hot bath.

That was the only hot bath we had, so we were all glad when the weather got warm enough that we could bathe in cold water.

We received our first Red Cross package in Japan on April 3rd. The contents were the same as in those we received at Las Piñas. This provided a welcome addition to our diet. We tried to string out the eating of the contents to make them last a while.

According to my notes, a Japanese worker told one of our men on April 14th that President Roosevelt had died the day before at 4:00 AM I don't know what time zone he was using.

On April 15th, they started to give us a second Red Cross box and found twenty-four boxes missing. They kept us all standing outside all morning until finally, the men who took them confessed, and most of the stuff was recovered. Seven men were involved, and they were all new men who came in from a camp near Tokyo on March 31st. The men who had stolen the boxes didn't get any and had to do time in the guard house on rice and water. I don't remember how long they were in the guardhouse.

On June 28th, a group of forty-five Australian officers arrived in camp. We enjoyed talking to them, and they had good news about the progress of the war. One evening, a group of us gathered in the compound, and one of the Australian officers, who was a pilot and was shot down much later than when the rest of us became prisoners, sang "White Christmas" for us. We had not heard it before, of course.

There were quite a few air raids in July near enough for us to hear the bombs. We could hear the Japanese talking about the "B niju ku" (B-29s). We had never seen one. One day, we could hear shelling much of the day. On the night of August 14th, there were heavy bombing raids. We could hear the bombing.

On August 15th, the Japanese in the town gathered and received a public address by some official.

In my notes, I wrote, "August 16th and 17th, no work, rumors the war is over, inclined to believe it."

On August 18th, a Japanese, who was making some repairs in our kitchen, said the war was over. One of the Australian officers who could read Japanese offered him some money if he would bring him a newspaper reporting the war was over. He brought one the next day, and we were all elated. However, we had become such emotional zombies, that there was no demonstration of any kind.

That evening, a quartet of Australian officers sang the song "Soldiers' (Prisoners') Farewell," which they had collaborated in writing that afternoon. I got a copy from one of them and copied it into my booklet. That was the last poem I collected.

On August 20, 1945, the Japanese camp commander called an assembly and announced that America and Japan had reached an agreement ending the war. He said he hoped we would stay in camp for our own protection because some of the Japanese civilians might still have hard feelings.

The Japanese gave us a radio so we could listen to the American Armed Forces news broadcasts. They kept announcing from General Eichelberger's headquarters that all prisoners of war should stay where they were. We should not try to go to our armed forces. They would come to us or send for us when they were prepared to handle us.

On August 28th, some carrier planes located our camp. One buzzed the camp and threw out a note asking, "Have you received your rations yet?" One of the men went into the kitchen where they had a sack of lime, and wrote "NO" in large letters on the ground. The planes then started diving down and flying low over the camp to drop a crate of K-rations. The trouble was that a crate would probably weigh forty pounds, and they came down with a pretty high velocity. We had to watch and get out of the way. I saw one coming at me, and I jumped under the covered walkway and stood near a post. The crate hit right over my head, knocked a couple of boards off, and bounced off onto the ground.

Unfortunately, one of the Australian officers was inside his barracks lying in a top bunk when one of these crates dropped through the bark roof and hit him right in the chest. It killed him instantly.

Later that day, several B-29s flew over and dropped large amounts of supplies. There were new khaki uniforms in addition to all kinds of canned food and other non-perishable food. These supplies were packed in large drums made by welding two fifty-five gallon steel drums together end to end. The open end was closed by means of a wooden head tied on with rope. They made a harness for the drums of large rope about one and one half inches in diameter, and they were tied to parachutes. These were stowed in the bomb bays of the B-29s. The bomb bays were opened, and the drums were released from them, just as if they were bombs. It was tragic that some of these drums broke the ties when the parachutes opened, and they came down like bombs. The crews had aimed the drops so they would land in or near the camp. Again, those of us who were watching managed to get out of the way of the two or three drums that broke loose. However, Bill Fisher, a likable guy from Missouri, was inside a barracks when one came through the roof and killed him instantly.

One of the men grabbed the sack of lime, and wrote on the ground, "Drop Outside, 2 men killed." Most of the men in camp then went outside the camp to a shelter the Japanese had dug into the mountainside, and most of us got in there until the drops were completed.

I don't know if anyone in the planes could read the message on the ground from the altitude at which they were flying, but another flight came on August 30th, and they flew a path so the supplies dropped in the valley just below the camp. We then went out and rolled the drums up the hill to camp.

We dug two graves just a short way outside the camp entrance and buried the two men who were killed. They were the only two prisoners that I know of who died in Japan who were not cremated. We had only one other man die in this camp. His name was Gravitt, and he died from pneumonia back in March, I think. Anyway, it was before spring.

The deaths of these two men really bothered me, due to the fact that they had withstood all the hardships and hell the Japanese had subjected them to for three and a half years or more, and then lost their lives after the war was over and before they could go home.

There were several other prisoners killed after they were liberated, and before they got back to the U.S. To me, these deaths were really illustrative of how unfair life can be.

On September 22, 1945, the Japanese police (all of our army guards had taken off for parts unknown) escorted us down to the train station where we boarded a train which took us to a seaport. I think it was Sendai. There the navy met us. After some questioning, we were put on a landing craft (I think it was an LCVP [Landing Craft Vehicle and Personnel]) and ferried out to the naval hospital ship, *Rescue*. On the landing craft, we were given coffee, and it seemed amazing that we could put all the sugar and canned milk in it that we wanted.

When we got to the hospital ship, as we walked up the gang-way we were told to take off all of our clothing and throw it into the water. It bothered me to take off the brand new khaki uniforms that had been dropped to us and throw them away. As we stepped onto the ship, we were given disposable cups of some kind to hold over our eyes, and we were liberally doused with DDT powder. Then we went directly to the showers, took a good shower, and were issued new uniforms. Our barracks bags were sprayed with some kind of disinfectant, and we were shown to our bunks. We spent the night on this ship. Everything was so clean, and we were treated so well, that it finally soaked in that we were back in good hands and, like Scarlett O'Hara, we would never go hungry again.

Note to the Reader:

After World War II, Bishop McKendree attended The University of Texas in Austin, and earned a B.S. degree in petroleum engineering in February, 1952.

While at the University, he met Beverly Jean Biery, who was completing the MA degree in clinical psychology at U.T. Austin. They were married June 7, 1952.

After graduation, Bishop worked for Gulf Oil Corporation in the oil fields of West Texas for approximately ten years as a petroleum production engineer. He resigned that position and accepted employment with the Texas Railroad Commission as a petroleum engineer in the Oil and Gas Division, retiring in 1987. He and his wife, Beverly, still reside in Austin, Texas.

They raised three children.

The oldest, a son, Alan, earned a B.A. in mathematics from Trinity University in San Antonio, Texas, and a B.A. in drama from U.T. Austin. He lives in Austin and works for a computer consortium there.

The second child, Jean E. McKendree, received a Ph.D. in cognitive psychology from Carnegie Mellon University and now resides in York, U.K., with her husband, John Mateer. She heads a psychological research project based at York University.

The youngest child, Edith M. Shipley, received a B.A. in psychology and a B.M. in music history from Oberlin College and Conservatory of Music. She now lives in Barrington, New Hampshire, with her husband, Christopher. They, with a partner, are founders of North Coast Software Corporation, and Edith also gives private lessons in voice and piano.

Glossary

This list was prepared at the suggestion of people who have read these poems and who have never been in the Philippines or in any branch of the armed services. I hope it will be useful in helping people better understand the meanings of some of the poems.

Abucay—a small town (barrio) near the east coast of Bataan Peninsula in the northern half.

B.C.—Battery Commander.

Balanga—a town near the east coast of Bataan in the east central area.

Bango—Japanese word for count, or roll call.

Brother Quezon—refers to President Manuel Quezon, who was president of the Philippines at that time and came to Corregidor when Manila was evacuated. He later was evacuated to the U.S. where he died before the war was over.

C.P.—Command Post.

Cabanatuan—Cabanatuan Prison Camp No. 1. Prisoner-of-war camp near the city of Cabanatuan in the north central part of the island of Luzon in the Philippines.

Carabao—water buffalo native to the Philippines.

Co-prosperity—refers to what the Japanese called "The Greater East Asia Co-Prosperity Sphere," which they were going to establish after they conquered China, Indochina, the Malay Peninsula, the South Pacific Islands, and Australia.

D.S.C.'s—Distinguished Service Crosses.

Dewey—Admiral Dewey's defeat of the Spanish fleet in Manila Bay in the Spanish-American War (1898), which resulted in the U.S. obtaining control of the Philippine Islands.

Garand—the Garand (M-1) rifle. It was the modern infantry rifle at that time. The U.S. Army 31st Infantry Regiment was the only regiment on Bataan which was equipped with the Garand.

H. E.—abbreviation for "high explosive."

Hacienda Road—road from Abucay to Abucay Hacienda in the foothills of Mt. Natib in northeastern Bataan.

Head—navy term for rest room. Same as "latrine" in the army.

Honcho—Japanese word for foreman, or supervisor.

Kiotski—Japanese command which is the same as the U.S. Army command "Attention."

Kuda—Japanese word expressing anger or dissatisfaction.

Limay—a small town (barrio) on the east coast of Bataan in the southern half.

Lingayen—Lingayen Gulf, where the Japanese landed their largest force on the island of Luzon at the beginning of the war.

Mariveles Mountain—a high mountain on the southern end of Bataan.

Motors in the west—Most of the air attacks on Corregidor were made by planes approaching from over the China Sea to the west of Bataan and Corregidor. The first warning we would get would be "motors in the west."

Nippy—slang for Nipponese, or Japanese.

Nipa—a type of palm which grows in the Philippines, the leaves of which are used to make thatch for the roofs of native shacks. Sometimes it is also used for the sides of the shacks.

One-five-five—refers to a 155 mm. artillery piece used by the field artillery.

P-Forties—P-40 fighter planes, the most modern fighter planes in the Philippines at that time. Only a few survived after the early air battles and the retreat into Bataan. They operated from a hastily constructed air strip near the town of Cabcaben on the southern end of Bataan.

Quinauan—a point of land on the west coast of Bataan where one of the battles was fought in what came to be known as the "Battle of the Points."

Q.M.C.—Quartermaster Corps.

Quan—a Philippine Tagalog word meaning an unknown quantity, entity, or condition. Actually, the Tagalog spelling is "kwan." The Americans in prison who had cans they could cook in dubbed them "Quan Cans," since often the ingredients were strange; how they would taste as well as their nutritional value were often unknown.

Republic—a former passenger liner which had been converted to a troop transport ship.

The Rock—the name by which soldiers stationed in the Philippines referred to the island of Corregidor. The official Army name for Corregidor was Fort Mills.

Samat—Mt. Samat is a mountain in the south central part of Bataan where a major battle was fought during the final days before the fall of Bataan (April 9, 1942).

S.S.C.'s—Silver Star Citations.

Scuttlebutts—nautical slang for rumor or gossip. Sometimes shortened to "scuttle."

Shooting butts in a holder—Prisoners who smoked soon fashioned cigarette holders from pieces of bamboo or other materials so that one could smoke cigarette butts of others without putting them in one's mouth. Also, the entire cigarette could be smoked; cigarettes were very scarce at times.

Tojo—Premier Hideki Tojo, wartime premier of Japan.

Tunnel rats—men who fought the war from the safety of tunnels.

Zero—the best Japanese fighter plane in WW II.

CORNELL EAST ASIA SERIES

No. 75 *Barbed Wire and Rice: Poems and Songs from Japanese Prisoner-of-War Camps,* collected by Bishop D. McKendree

FORTHCOMING

The Gods Come Dancing: A Study of the Japanese Ritual Dance of Yamabushi Kagura, by Irit Averbuch

Restless Spirits: Noh Plays from the Fourth Category, Parallel Translations with Running Commentary, by Chifumi Shimazaki

Singing Like a Cricket: Hooting Like an Owl, Selected Poems by Yi Kyu-bo, translated by Kevin O'Rourke

Back to Heaven: Selected Poems by Chon Sang Pyong, translated by Brother Anthony of Taizé and Young-Moo Kim

For ordering information, please contact the Cornell East Asia Series, East Asia Program, Cornell University, 140 Uris Hall, Ithaca, NY 14853-7601, USA; phone (607) 255-6222, fax (607) 255-1388.

Barbed Wire and Rice
Poems and Songs
from Japanese Prisoner-of-War Camps
Collected by Bishop D. McKendree

Bishop McKendree's gathering of poems and songs from Japanese prisoner-of-war camps in World War II is the remarkable outcome of a brutal experience. The materials were elusive in their circulation among the prisoners, dangerous to those who composed or performed them, and certainly would have been fatal to McKendree, had he been caught with them. They tell their stories, and Bishop McKendree his, in this book.

2-95/.2M cloth/.5M paper/TS